MW01010599

DEAR MEMORY

ALSO BY VICTORIA CHANG

Poetry

Asian American Poetry: The Next Generation (editor)

Circle

Salvinia Molesta

The Boss

Barbie Chang

OBIT

Children's books

Is Mommy? (illustrated by Marla Frazee)

Love, Love

DEAR MEMORY

Letters on

Writing, Silence,

and Grief

VICTORIA CHANG

MILKWEED EDITIONS

© 2021, Text and art by Victoria Chang
All rights reserved. Except for brief quotations in critical articles or reviews, no part of this book may be reproduced in any manner without prior written permission from the publisher: Milkweed Editions, 1011 Washington Avenue South, Suite 300, Minneapolis, Minnesota 55415.
(800) 520-6455
milkweed.org

Published 2021 by Milkweed Editions
Printed in Canada
Cover design by Mary Austin Speaker
Cover art by Victoria Chang
Author photo by Issac Fitzgerald
21 22 23 24 25 5 4 3 2 1
First Edition

Milkweed Editions, an independent nonprofit publisher, gratefully acknowledges sustaining support from the Alan B. Slifka Foundation and its president, Riva Ariella Ritvo-Slifka; the Ballard Spahr Foundation; *Copper Nickel*; the Jerome Foundation; the McKnight Foundation; the National Endowment for the Arts; the National Poetry Series; the Target Foundation; and other generous contributions from foundations, corporations, and individuals. Also, this activity is made possible by the voters of Minnesota through a Minnesota State Arts Board Operating Support grant, thanks to a legislative appropriation from the arts and cultural heritage fund. For a full listing of Milkweed Editions supporters, please visit milkweed.org.

Library of Congress Cataloging-in-Publication Data

Names: Chang, Victoria, 1970- author.
Title: Dear memory : letters on writing, silence, and grief / by Victoria Chang.
Description: First edition. | Minneapolis, Minnesota : Milkweed Editions, 2021. | Summary:
    "From National Book Award-longlisted poet Victoria Chang, a collection of literary letters and
    mementos on the art of remembering across generations"-- Provided by publisher.
Identifiers: LCCN 2021007010 (print) | LCCN 2021007011 (ebook) | ISBN 9781571313928
    (hardcover) | ISBN 9781571317360 (ebook)
Classification: LCC PS3603.H3575 D43 2021 (print) | LCC PS3603.H3575 (ebook) | DDC
    816/.6--dc23
LC record available at https://lccn.loc.gov/2021007010
LC ebook record available at https://lccn.loc.gov/2021007011

Milkweed Editions is committed to ecological stewardship. We strive to align our book production practices with this principle, and to reduce the impact of our operations in the environment. We are a member of the Green Press Initiative, a nonprofit coalition of publishers, manufacturers, and authors working to protect the world's endangered forests and conserve natural resources. *Dear Memory* was printed on acid-free 10% postconsumer-waste paper by Friesens Corporation.

For my mother and father,
my grandparents, great-grandparents . . .

The sense of mortality—our own, but also that of those we most love—doesn't only cast us backward. It also propels imagination forward.

—Christian Wiman, *He Held Radical Light*

There are no stars tonight but those of memory. Yet how much room for memory there is in the loose girdle of soft rain.

—Hart Crane, from "My Grandmother's Love Letters"

DEAR MEMORY

• Mother, Sister, and me •

Dear Mother,

I have so many questions. What city were you born in? What was your American birthday? Your Chinese birthday? What did your mother do? What did your grandmother do? Who was your father, grandfather? It's too late now. But I would like to know.

I would like to know why your mother followed Chiang Kai-shek, taking you and your six (or seven?) siblings across China to Taiwan. I would like to know what was said in the planning meeting. I would like to know who was in that meeting. Where that meeting took place.

I would like to know the people who were left behind. I would like to know if there are other people who look like me.

I would like to know if you took a train. If you walked. If you had pockets in your dress. If you wore pants. If your hand was in a fist, if you held a small stone. I would like to know if you thought the trees were black or green at night, if it was cold enough to see your breath, to sting your fingers. I would like to know who you spoke to along the way. If you had some preserved salty plums, which we both love, in your pocket.

I would like to know if you carried a bag. If you had a book in your bag. I would like to know where you got your food for the trip. Why I never knew your mother, father, or your siblings. I would like to have known your father. I would like to know what his voice sounded like. If it was brittle or pale. If it was blue or red. I would like to know the sound he made when he swallowed food.

I would like to know if your mother was afraid. During college, I spent several weeks with her in Taiwan. She bought me bao zi, buns, every morning—the bao that steamed in small plastic bags with no ties, and sweet dou jiang, tofu milk. Always too hot for me to drink. She sat there and watched me eat, complained to me about your brother's wife. Complained of being sick and how no one would help her.

Do you know how long it took me to figure out how to call an ambulance? And then when they came, she refused to go. I still remember how the two men stared at me, as if I could move a country.

Listen. It's the wind. That's the same wind from your countries. Sometimes if I listen closely at night, I can hear you drop a small bag at the door. I hear the sound of the bao touching the ground and the wind trying to open the bag.

But when I open the door, there's nothing there. Just the same wind. Thousands of years old. Happy birthday, wind. Happy birthday, Mother. April 6, 1940. I know this now. All the nurses, doctors, and morticians asked me, so I memorized it, your American birthday. *April 6, 1940,* I said again and again. As if I had known this my whole life.

The shape of memory is   a tree. The trees have

Witnessed all the wars.

What is a tree but

persistence and secrets?

· Mother ·

生在本校 高中部 修業期

滿式頷及格准予 第一條

中華民國肆 柒年 柒月 日

ME: WHAT DID YOUR FATHER DO?

MOTHER: HE WAS IN THE KMT [KUOMINTANG] MILITARY.

ME: DOING WHAT?

MOTHER: TRANSPORTATION STUFF.

ME: DO YOU HAVE FAMILY LEFT IN CHINA?

MOTHER: YES. MY COUSIN'S FAMILY. WE IN THE JIN FAMILY HAD MORE MONEY THAN THEM.

MOTHER: MY MOTHER ASKED THEM TO GO BUT THEY WOULDN'T.

MOTHER: THEY STAYED IN CHINA.

規定

業肄中學法 畢業證書

· Mother ·

Dear Grandmother,

Today I found a Certificate of Marriage and a translation of it by the President Translation Service. The date is July 26, 1939. Now I know your name: Miss Chang Chi-Yin. I also know you were twenty-seven and Grandfather twenty-six. I wonder if this was considered strange at the time, your being older than him.

I now know you were born on April 29, 1913. Seeing this date makes me cry. The tears are long and rusted. I have tried to tie them together into a long string toward your country. The farthest I've ever made it was Kansas. The tornadoes always break my tears.

Dear Grandmother, I now know you were born in Chingwan Hsien, Hopei Province. I google Hopei and see it is in the North of China, where all the good doughy food Mother used to make comes from—the bao zi, jiao zi, and shao bing. I can see how close you were to Beijing and Mongolia.

I learn that you were born one year after the Qing dynasty collapsed. I learn that you lived amid civil war. I wonder if this is why you took your children and left for Taiwan.

I can't find your town, Chingwan Hsien, on Google because it's probably spelled another way. After more searching, I figure out it is likely Jing Wan Xian. But I still can't locate it on the map of Hopei, which I figure out is also Hebei Province.

The Certificate says you were united in matrimony at Chungking City, Szechuan Province. Google says there are thirty million people there. I try to imagine thirty million people who look like me. In that moment, grief freezes.

The Certificate says you were introduced to each other by Mr. Chang Kan-Chen and Mrs. Chou Chi-Ying. I wonder who these people were. I wonder if yours was an arranged marriage or if you loved each other. Or both. I wonder what love looked like in China in 1939.

The Certificate says: *These two parties are now united forever in harmony on this auspicious day in taking an oath of mutual fidelity throughout their lives.* What happened afterwards, I don't know. I do know that when I met you, the one time I met you, you were no longer together and hadn't been in a long time. But Mother never talked about that. Mother only ever bitterly talked about how you favored all of your sons.

The one time I met your former spouse, my grandfather, was when Mother brought me to the arcade to meet him. I played Ms. Pac-Man the whole time, while they stood near the door and talked. Their mouths moved but I couldn't hear anything. All I remember is the sound of the yellow mouth eating white pellets.

I often think about what the poet Mary Jo Bang wrote about her dead son, *What is elegy but the attempt / To rebreathe life / Into what the gone once was / Before he grew to enormity.*[i] That is what Mother feels like: an enormity. My history feels even larger. The size of atmosphere.

An elegy reflects on the loss of a loved one. What form can express the loss of something you never knew but knew existed? Lands you never knew? People? Can one experience such a loss? The last definition of absence is *the nonexistence or lack of.* See how the *of* hangs there like someone about to jump off a balcony?

I want to believe in the origin story. I want to believe we all desire to know how we came to be, who we came from. I want to know why my fingers are so long, why my mouth naturally frowns, why my back has chronic pain, why I have freckles all over my nose. Why my mind is so restless.

But what if, during her own migration, my mother's memories migrated, too, and became exiled from their origins? What if both my origin and memory can never be pinned down?

Grandmother, in the list of people present during your marriage, there were two matchmakers, three parents, and a witness. Where was the fourth parent? I now know the names of three of my ancestors: Jin Hsuan-San, Chang Yen-Chen, Pi Pao-Chuan. I also have a photocopy of the original marriage certificate in Chinese. I now know your names in Chinese characters, though I can't read them well.

My mother had a photocopy of each of these documents. And then she made another copy of the copies. So many copies to forget her past. If I throw them away, does that mean I was never born? In some ways, being born Chinese in America means not being born at all.

Maybe all of our memories are tied to the memories of others. Maybe my memories are tied to Mother's memories, and Mother's memories are like objects in a mirror—I see them, but I can't ever reach them. When Mother died, my exile detached from her exile, and that gap filled with longing.

But with these papers, there's now a new wind. A Mongolian wind from the North, one I have never smelled before. A new feeling that I, too, come from something, from some people, from somewhere.

CERTIFICATE OF MARRIAGE

TRANSLATION

Date   : July 26, 1939

Mr. JIN PAO-LAN, a native of Hsiangho Hsien, Hopei Province,
26 of age, born on April 10, 1914; Miss CHANG CHI-YIN, a native
of Chingwan Hsien, Hopei Province, 27 of age, born on April
29, 1913, were united in matrimony on 26th day of July, 1939 a.m.
at Chungking City, Szuchuan Province. They have been introduced
to each other by Mr. CHANG KAN-CHEN and Mrs. CHOU CHI-YING, and
the wedding ceremony was officiated by Mr. LI CHIEN-MING. These
two parties are now united forever in harmony on this auspicious
day in taking an oath of mutual fidelity throughout their lives.
This certificate is hereby recorded.

Bridegroom	: JIN PAO-LAN	(sealed)
Bride	: CHANG CHI-YIN	(sealed)
Witness	: LI CHIEN-MING	(sealed)
Matchmakers	: CHANG KAN-CHEN	(sealed)
	CHOU CHI-YING	(sealed)
Parents	: JIN HSUAN-SAN	(sealed)
	CHANG YEN-CHEN	(sealed)
	PI PAO-CHUAN	(sealed)

本文件及附組文件之簽名或蓋章，經
中華民國台灣台北地方法院公證處
公証人認証。   公証人蔡長郎
Attested on this 5th day January
19__, at the Taiwan Taipe District
Court, Republic of China, That the
signatures/seals in this/attached
documents are authentic
Jen Tzu
No.
81056   Tsng Ing-lang
             Notary Public   PRESIDENT TRANSLATION SERVICE
                              P.O. Box 7199, CHANGCHUN RD., TAIPEI
                    I CERTIFY THAT THIS TRANSLATION IS A TRUE
                    AND CORRECT ENGLISH VERSION OF THE ATTACHED
                    ORIGINAL, TO THE BEST OF MY KNOWLEDGE AND
                    BELIEF.
                                        TRANSLATOR:

JAN. 7 . 1982

統 一 翻 譯 社
President Translation Service

南京總社	長春社	北門社	敦化社	信義社	信陽社
南京東路2段30號3樓	長春路146號3樓	延平南路20號2樓	敦化南路396巷49號2樓	信義路三段126號2樓	信陽街5-2號2樓
Tel: 5116092. 5629234 5116404. 5629239 5313030. 5621414	Tel:5624577. 5813078 5222002	Tel: 3615632. 3117077	Tel: 7114577. 7114866 7710303 7116612	Tel: 7053985 7043834	Tel: 3314697. 3716245 3111164.3719542 3316796

GRANDMOTHER WHO LEFT CHINA

Everything but the flowers

and books are cut off.

History has been narrowed

down so much that

GRANDMOTHER'S SISTER WHO STAYED IN CHINA

I can no longer get in.

• Maternal Grandmother and Grandfather •

Dear Silence,

I wrote in the margins of my notebook: *What are you doing? What's at stake here? Why are you skirting around things? Why are you circling around and around, afraid to go into the center?* I think I am circling around you, Silence, your center, and the closer I get, the closer I am to shame, to the language of shame.

The center could be the *rack* that Mary Ruefle speaks of in her book *Madness, Rack, and Honey.* The *torment, pain, torture* of what *poetry does to the world, what poets do with words, and what words will do to a poet.*[ii] I don't think, though, that Ruefle meant that we should only write about painful life experiences or feelings, but rather that we should write to put language at risk. I like that: *What words will do to a poet.*

Do I want to risk going into you in order to come out with words? To let the words build into something that is no longer me? Can I be the hawk and the storm that tries to kill the hawk? Am I willing to write about the dead? Will the language that I make murder me?

In our house, loud language was everywhere—bundles of Mandarin from Mother's mouth, Father's nearly perfect English but Taiwanese-accented Mandarin. Then our Chinglish. But in our house, silence arranged itself like furniture. I was always bumping into it. When unrelated aunties and uncles came over for dinner parties, I envied the laughing as they drank Riunite wine, ate steaming fish and tofu. When they left, they took all the words. What was left after their laughter was always my grief.

I didn't know what was wrong so each night I prayed to God, but God just gave me tomorrow. Eventually, I stopped praying because I realized that God and I did not speak the same language.

Last night, I went to the talent show at the children's school. Kids dressed as sharks running around in circles. Popular girls with matching ripped jeans and long flat-ironed hair singing pop songs and dancing unenthusiastically. A magic show, piano players, ukulele players, joke-tellers . . .

Then a boy got up and the music began. He sang "Never Enough" from the film *The Greatest Showman*. I didn't remember the song or the film, but his opening breath was so quiet, it was Ruefle's *rack*. That was poetry. I think that is why I write. That is why I want to make art.

After he finished to a standing ovation, I remembered that this was the boy who was recently outed at school. This small seventh-grader sent his insides out, through his mouth, in small envelopes.

I am seeking whatever is painful in my body, whatever is joyful. While seeking, I may never find myself. While seeking, I have no idea what form I may take or whether anyone, including myself, will ever like what I write. Most of writing feels like walking in the dark. I'm reminded of what Donald Barthelme said: *The writer is that person who, embarking upon her task, does not know what to do.*[iii]

Recently, during a reading, the poet Valzhyna Mort said, *Lacking language is the beginning of a poem to me*. This is what writing feels like to me too. In some ways we are coming out of silence to make a new language. This making comes out of a deep desire to understand something that is invisible and voiceless.

Do you know that Jeanette Winterson cast this generative uncertainty of creative practice in terms of time in *Art Objects: Essays on Ecstasy and Effrontery*:

My work is rooted in silence. It grows out of deep beds of con-
templation, where words, which are living things, can form and
re-form into new wholes. What is visible, the finished books, are
underpinned by the fertility of unaccounted hours. A writer has
no use for the clock. A writer lives in an infinity of days, time
without end, ploughed under.[iv]

Writing feels like being within you, silence, and then emerging, bronzed. Somehow, writing feels more related to beginnings than endings. Writing feels outside of time. In a windowless room. Not in a room at all. In a state of being half-awake and half-possessed. In an endless snowstorm, *ploughed under.* Alone. As I reach for memory that has become extinct.

Dear Silence, how do I enter you, seeking answers, but come out writing into and toward ambiguity? How do I *live the questions,* as Rilke says in *Letters to a Young Poet.* How many times have I looked so hard for someone's eyes to catch mine that I disappeared? That feels like writing. That feels like living the question.

It's not that the boy's voice sits within me now. It's the bird his voice became that I now seek. I am trying to make birds out of silence. Birds that will fly away, that I will never see die.

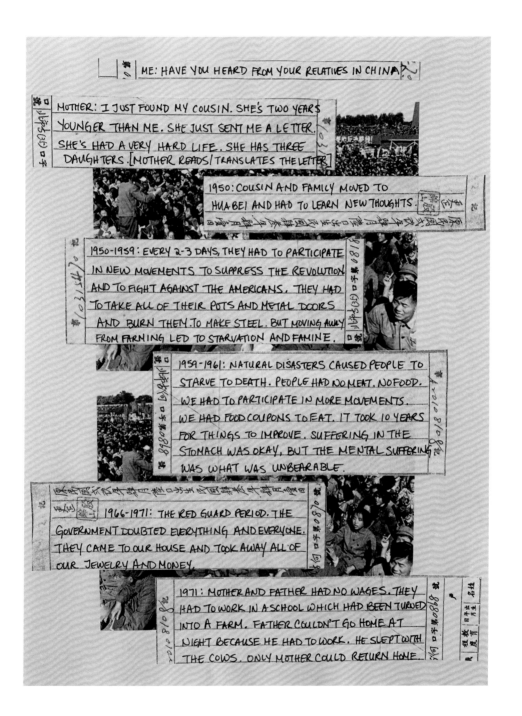

ME: HAVE YOU HEARD FROM YOUR RELATIVES IN CHINA?

MOTHER: I JUST FOUND MY COUSIN. SHE'S TWO YEARS YOUNGER THAN ME. SHE JUST SENT ME A LETTER. SHE'S HAD A VERY HARD LIFE. SHE HAS THREE DAUGHTERS. [MOTHER READS/TRANSLATES THE LETTER]

1950: COUSIN AND FAMILY MOVED TO HUABEI AND HAD TO LEARN NEW THOUGHTS.

1950-1959: EVERY 2-3 DAYS, THEY HAD TO PARTICIPATE IN NEW MOVEMENTS TO SUPPRESS THE REVOLUTION AND TO FIGHT AGAINST THE AMERICANS. THEY HAD TO TAKE ALL OF THEIR POTS AND METAL DOORS AND BURN THEM TO MAKE STEEL. BUT MOVING AWAY FROM FARMING LED TO STARVATION AND FAMINE.

1959-1961: NATURAL DISASTERS CAUSED PEOPLE TO STARVE TO DEATH. PEOPLE HAD NO MEAT. NO FOOD. WE HAD TO PARTICIPATE IN MORE MOVEMENTS. WE HAD FOOD COUPONS TO EAT. IT TOOK 10 YEARS FOR THINGS TO IMPROVE. SUFFERING IN THE STOMACH WAS OKAY, BUT THE MENTAL SUFFERING WAS WHAT WAS UNBEARABLE.

1966-1971: THE RED GUARD PERIOD. THE GOVERNMENT DOUBTED EVERYTHING AND EVERYONE. THEY CAME TO OUR HOUSE AND TOOK AWAY ALL OF OUR JEWELRY AND MONEY.

1971: MOTHER AND FATHER HAD NO WAGES. THEY HAD TO WORK IN A SCHOOL WHICH HAD BEEN TURNED INTO A FARM. FATHER COULDN'T GO HOME AT NIGHT BECAUSE HE HAD TO WORK. HE SLEPT WITH THE COWS. ONLY MOTHER COULD RETURN HOME.

• *Mother's Cousin's letter* •

Dear Grandfather,

I remember meeting you only once. You could only speak Taiwanese so we sat in Uncle's apartment in Taipei while you nodded and smiled because I can't understand Taiwanese. I could see your gold teeth. You were a landscape filled with general trees, general grass, general sky.

I heard that you died when you fell in the bathroom, broke a hip. I imagine you on the ground in the corner of a small apartment, next to a general toilet, in a general bathroom.

I recently found an *Affidavits* in a box. The top part, an English translation:

> This is to certify that, to my best recollection, Mr. Shih-tou CHANG was legitimately married to Mrs. Fong-mei LEE-CHANG in Taipei, Taiwan, in winter, 1938, after his first wife died of illness in summer, 1935.

> Mr. Shih-tou CHANG's first wife bore no child but legitimately adopted a girl named Yei-pin in 1932.

I was surprised to read that you had a first wife. I wonder who she was. I wonder what she died of. Now I know I have another aunt, named Yei-pin. I wonder where she was adopted from. I wonder what happened to her parents. Was she from an affair or from another marriage? I wonder how she knew your first wife, whether you raised her, what she looks like, whether she is still alive.

Grandfather, do you remember when your second wife, Father's mother, came to America when she was ill? I still remember how suddenly she appeared. I don't know how long she stayed, but she was always in bed and it was always dark. I think it was liver cancer, but does it matter? I've never seen Grandmother stand up. I wonder how tall she was.

Recently, I found a photo of us together on a rusted Ferris wheel where I looked happy and she didn't look sick at all. Perhaps that's the first time I had met her. Perhaps I have seen her stand up before. Perhaps something never happened if no one remembers it. On the back of the photo are some Chinese characters I can't read. Perhaps something never happened if no one can read the label. Perhaps there's no truth. Just memory and words.

One day Grandmother's picture sat on a bureau, two small bowls of rice on each side, incense sticks upright and burning. I've only smelled that scent a few more times—at a temple, in a general Chinatown in a general city. A smoking sweetness not of this land.

I don't know how long those sticks burned for, but it seemed like a few winters. Now, I realize she may have already been in hospice and may have only lived in our house for a few months, or even a few weeks, like a bird passing through but dying in a foreign land.

Where were you at this time, Grandfather? Why didn't you come? I wonder whether there was a funeral and, if there was, who was watching me. Maybe she returned to Taiwan and was buried there.

I wonder why any of this matters, why it matters now, why I haven't wondered more about this before. Because I was supposed to be lucky. Father and Mother were supposed to be lucky.

Lucky people are supposed to live in the future.

The cost of being so lucky is that you never learn how to acknowledge pain. Because you're always lucky, you should always appreciate being alive, what you have. Nothing should ever be wrong, go wrong. The problem is that the space between how you really feel and luck is always shame.

Recently, I visited your son, Father, in his facility. I walked in on him standing in the bathroom. Sometime in the last few weeks, he had forgotten how to use the toilet.

When I took Father downstairs to the patio, he stood by a plant and put his arms out in front of him, as if willing it to grow. I watched him lean into the plant and then away, back and forth. From afar, he looked like he was doing Tai Chi.

I wonder what kind of craggy twigs still exist in his brain. It's hard to watch someone who used to have a switchblade as a mind finally kneel down. Yesterday, I showed him a picture of your dead wife. His normally glazed eyes looked, and he said, *Ma ma*. Then his eyes began to water. Maybe our final memory will be of our mothers.

When Father was stronger, I once handed him a basketball and told him to shoot it into the hole in front of him. After about six tries, one went in and we all cheered. Then another, and we cheered again, jumping up and down. My own voice startled me, its Americanness. Its loudness. Its confidence. The sicker Father gets, the more American I become.

Maybe our desire for the past grows after the decay of our present. When the present is more than we can hold, it turns into history. And the future turns into water. The water between your countries.

There's a buzzing in my ears now. Where there once was silence, now there is lightheadedness. And no one to answer all the questions I've never had before.

When people leave a country, they leave everything. The land, the smells, the people. The objective is simple: to build a better life, without the incisions of the past. A family tree ended. People no longer sleep beside one another. Time stops and a new time begins. The two never cross.

What Srđja Pavlović wrote must be true: *Those of us displaced indeed live in a moment that lasts a lifetime.*[V]

Grandfather, I fear your son will join you soon. I hope there isn't such a thing as your heaven and our heaven. I hope Father can meet you in the one borderless afterlife. I hope he won't have to travel to see you. I hope there are no suitcases there. No more packing. No more migrants. No more caravans. One language.

I hope when Father sees you, his words will return. I hope then Father can tell you about the sixty years that you missed, and maybe when I see you both, I can ask you about your first wife and Yei-pin.

AFFIDAVITS

This is to certify that, to my best recollection, Mr. Shih-tou CHANG was legitimately married to Mrs. Fong-mei LEE-CHANG in Taipei, Taiwan, in winter, 1938, after his first wife died of illness in summer, 1935.

Mr. Shih-tou CHANG's first wife bore no child but legitimately adopted a girl named Yei-pin in 1932.

Mr. Shih-tou CHANG and Mrs. Fong-mei LEE-CHANG have had five children since their marriage. All are legitimated in the Household Registration. Their names are : Fu-shueng CHANG, Li-hwa LEE, Shan-nan LEE, Jin-lien CHANG, Bi-lien CHANG.

The reason I am familiar with and willing to certify the above information is because Mr. & Mrs. CHANG and I have been close friends since our childhood. We all have been living in Taipei, and we have been keeping in contact.

Witness	: Ying CHOU-CHANG	Witness	: Yu-yen LEE-TSENG
Signature	*Ying Chou-Chang*	Signature	: *yu-yen Lee-Tseng*
Native Place	: Taipei City, China	Native Place	: Taoyuan Hsien, Taiwan, China
Date of Birth	: September 12, 1909	Date of China	: August 25, 1925
Address	: 2nd Fl., 62, Shuangho St., Taipei City, R. O. C.	Address	: 23, Lane 194, Sungchiang Rd., Taipei City, R. O. C.
Relationship	: Friend	Relationship	: Friend

證 明 書

1976,1,15

根據我的記憶，證此證明張石頭先生在一九三八年冬天與張李逢妹合法結婚於台北市。他的第一任夫人於一九三五年夏天因生病去世。

張石頭先生的第一任夫人未生子女，但在一九三二年合法的領養了一個女兒，名字叫月品。

張石頭先生與張李逢妹夫人生有五個子女；他們全部都合法地記載在戶籍登記簿上，他們的名字是：張富雄、李麗華、李善男、張金蓮、張碧蓮。

我熟悉而且願意證明以上資料的原因是因為張先生及夫人與我從小就是知已朋友。我們一直都住在台北市，並且時常來往。

證 明 人	：張周英	證 明 人	：曾李玉燕
簽　　名	：張周英	簽　　名	：曾李玉燕
籍　　貫	：台北市	籍　　貫	：台灣省桃園縣
生年月日	：1909年 9 月12日	生年月日	：1925年 8 月25日
地　　址	：台北市雙和街62號二樓	地　　址	：台北市松江路 194 巷23號
關　　係	：朋　友	關　　係	：朋　友

本文件之簽名及蓋章，經中華民國台灣台北地方法院公証處公証在証。

Attested on this 17th May, 1976, at the Taiwan Taipei District Court, Republic of China, That the signature(s)/seal(s) in this document is/are authentic.

Hsu Chia-lin

Jeny Tzu Ju. 35 , Signature of Notary Public

When the flames go out

you will disappear.

When someone lights

them again, I will appear

but weigh more.

· Paternal Grandfather on his ninety-second birthday ·

Dear D,

Do you remember those Fridays in gym class when Ms. A made us jog around the field behind the school? Did you know they tore down the school a few years ago? The school is charred, but the field isn't. The field is still there. The field foiled the trucks. The field won. My shadow is still in that field, attached to your shadow.

Do you remember how you used to run after me shouting, *You're so ugly!* How you would be in front of me, turn around and face me, jog backwards and laugh, *Why are you so ugly?* I yelled back at you with silence.

Dear D, I doubt you remember the fields, but the fields remember. I've wanted so many times to return to that field, to hear the grasses tell me what they heard.

Sometimes I wonder if you chased me one time or many times. I wonder how memory can become larger and larger. Does it matter whether you were wearing shorts or not? Whether the shorts had a stripe down each side? I imagine you had tube socks on. I imagine they had blue stripes. Sometimes I think of H, who once threw an icy snowball at my face. Did he do that once or every winter? And M, whenever we were alone, telling me to *go back to China*.

Sometimes I think about the styles of these bullies—some preferred to work alone, some needed an audience. But all of them had eyes that singed.

We often speak of memory as something that lingers, that returns again and again. Maybe memory is more like a homicide, each time it returns, it's a new memory, one that has murdered all the memories before.

Last night, we were driving in a car in Montana, a scientist and two poets. The scientist turned off the headlights by accident. All went black. And it was beautiful. For a moment, even trauma was gone. And then he found the switch, the lights came back on, and we were again driving underneath the fog, and all of my memories returned.

In that moment, in the darkness, it felt like I had seen Elizabeth Bishop's moose:

> Towering, antlerless,
> high as a church
> homely as a house
> . . .
> Why, why do we feel
> (we all feel) this sweet
> sensation of joy?[vi]

But in fact, I had seen nothing. In darkness, my body had emptied of all memories. In that moment, nothing had shape. Maybe Bishop's moose is death.

Dear D, a while back, I found you on Facebook. I saw two children with curly brown hair. You, like me, must teach your children how to be kind. You looked fit, like a runner. I imagined you running backward again. Step by step, able to shout and laugh at once, a small crowd gathering around you, all the same kids who are friends with me on Facebook now. How they looked on, some laughed.

Sarah was the only one who said anything. When she saw me crying in the locker room, she stopped, asked me if I was okay. Recently, Sarah messaged me and seemed to feel relief that I was still alive. Her concern startled me, as I had spent decades forgetting those early years, telling every new person I met that I had a great childhood. Because I had no history, history could be made, like a painting.

D, I wanted to send you a message and tell you about all the years your face stayed in my body, how you were that fog in Montana. Instead, I silently scrolled through your photos and looked at one where you stood next to Nina at a reunion and had captioned it *the one that got away.*

Sometimes I think I was the one who got away. From you, those kids, that quiet street on Langlewood Drive in Michigan. But then the fog. There's an eye in the middle of that fog.

In truth, I am ashamed to write this, to still think about the past, to still have these memories. I wonder if I am ashamed of the memories, the events, or myself. That fundamentally there was something wrong with me, my family, my countries I never knew.

Recently, I read about Nicole Chung's experiences being bullied in a mostly white town in her book, *All You Will Ever Know,* Cathy Park Hong's experiences being mocked on a school bus in *Minor Feelings,* Sejal Shah's experiences in *This Is One Way to Dance,* and Jaswinder Bolina's memories in *Of Color,* and my memories returned again, like Bishop's moose, *high as a church / homely as a house.* While reading, I suddenly felt less ashamed, less alone, and less silent.

Maybe memories are not to be forgotten but also not exactly to be remembered. Maybe that glorious, lumbering moose that stops us for a moment isn't death after all. Maybe it's memory, which is the exit wound of joy.

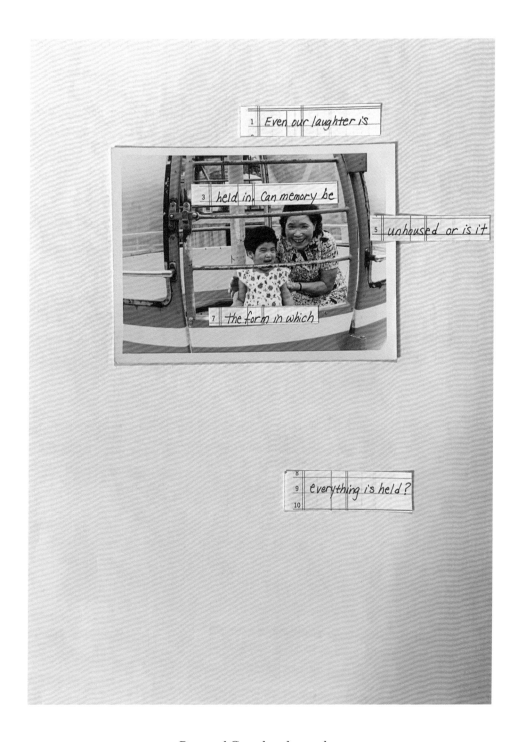

1 Even our laughter is

3 held in. Can memory be

5 unhoused or is it

7 the form in which

8
9 everything is held?
10

· Paternal Grandmother and me ·

Dear Mother,

I've been thinking about the Chinese restaurant, Dragon Inn, that we owned in Michigan. Was it in Rochester? I wish you could tell me where it was, what it was like, what it meant to you. I wish I could see its aerial view. Wish I could remember what was around it. Wish I could see what's there now. Another Chinese restaurant, a hair salon, ghosts?

Memory is everything, yet it is nothing. Memory is mine, but it is also clinging to the memory of others. Some of these others are dead. Or unable to speak, like Father.

Finding memories is a bit like free diving, although I've never free dived before. You jump in the water and hold your breath as long as you can without dying and hope you come up with a memory or two. Then there's the problem of opening the memory.

I remember that everything was red. The vinyl booths, the wallpaper, the lanterns, the sign in chop suey font with a dragon at the side. The big bowl of mints that tasted like toothpaste. The Chinese horoscope place mats. The beautiful chef with long black hair that he pulled into a ponytail.

This past week, I was in the Hudson Valley in New York. I walked out of the hotel and smelled garlic and sesame oil. The sign above said *Buddha Asian Bistro*. A new restaurant. Still the chop suey font. I turned away so as not to look inside, in the same way that I often turn my head away from Asian people on the street. If I don't look at them, I won't have to see myself.

I remember how crowded Dragon Inn was on Sundays when we had an all-you-can-eat brunch for $4.99. The line went out the door and everything was frenzied and nameless—the waitresses setting up, you lighting the little blue flames below the buffet containers, the chef shoveling fried rice into large metal containers, Father seating the customers who rushed in.

We offered fried rice, egg rolls, fried noodles, and maybe sweet and sour pork. I don't remember all the food. But people came from all over town, whatever town we were in.

One day, the brunch disappeared. I never asked why, but I imagine customers ate too much or it was too much work. These are the kinds of questions that absolutely did not matter at the time. The things that didn't matter at the time are often the most urgent questions after someone has died.

After the brunch disappeared, I remember the quiet restaurant with the handful of customers who came in occasionally for egg foo young or moo shu pork—none of the foods we ate. I remember our secret menu, the one just for Chinese people. This makes me think about how we perpetuate our own stereotypes, our own vanishing.

Resolve isn't inactive, though. Resolve is a live animal. We perpetuate the narrative that is given to us in order to survive. I didn't even know until recently that we opened restaurants because of labor restrictions placed on Chinese immigrants in the nineteenth century.

So much of our identity is based on how others expect us to be, how others want us to behave, to dress, to talk, how others perceive Chinese food. All the expectations, all the way down to the font. The alternative is to change the font and go out of business.

Once, a photographer asked me if I had a *Mao outfit* that I could wear for the magazine's shoot. I didn't even know what a *Mao outfit* was, if there was even such a thing. I'm not sure what I said or did, but I'm sure I didn't protest. *Can you wear all black then?* he asked. I thought about it, *Sure*. Because I thought a Chinese person should either say nothing or say *yes*.

Once the brunch disappeared, I spent my Sundays going back and forth to the liquor store next door. I remember having the urge to slip a small chunky chocolate square into my pocket without the owners noticing. I was so bored that I even missed the white people who lined up not to see us. Who lined up to eat us alive.

One day, the restaurant just disappeared. It may have had something to do with Father's having another job. Or with the restaurant's not making money. Or with the chefs always fighting with the waitstaff, who were always intentionally and stereotypically Chinese, not unlike the food itself.

Much later, I heard that you had bought the restaurant for your brother, whom you had sponsored from Taiwan, but he didn't want it or want to live in Michigan. I don't know which brother or where he is now.

When I google *Dragon Inn Rochester Michigan*, another Dragon Inn comes up, and I marvel at all the new Chinese restaurants such as Panda House, Pings, China Town . . . I wonder about all the Chinese American children wandering around those restaurants. I imagine the mother yelling *chi fan*, time to eat. And then all the kids gathering at the back table to eat dinner, a dinner that the chef made just for Chinese people. I'm not sure people even do this anymore. I don't remember the last time I saw a child in the back, slipping fortune cookies in small wax bags, like I did. Even the children have disappeared.

Now, instead of feeling ashamed of Chinese people, I yearn to be around them, the way plants have companions—the way garlic plants improve the growth and flavor of the beets next to them. Mother, you used to do all the ordering, but now when I go to a Chinese restaurant, sometimes I ask for the Chinese menu, something you often did. When I see an old Chinese woman at the table with her daughter, I see you, your garlic personality, my beet cheeks, and I proudly order everything you taught me to order. Maybe you had to die before I could ever order on my own, before I could have ever wanted to be Chinese.

Look at your arm.
You must have had
vitiligo. Even now our
eyes can't meet. But if
I look hard enough, I am
sitting on the ground,
in front of you, legs crossed,
just beyond where your
eyes are looking, and in a
moment, you will look up
and not see me.

• *Paternal Grandmother (center)* •

Dear Body,

Have you ever wondered when I would let you go? When I would let you simply sit in the field, fall backward, and match your shadow? If I lie down and outline myself with chalk, would you let me make you thinner? Last week, I read about how girls from families with higher academic achievement are at greater risk for anorexia. I don't remember when I started hating food.

Body, do you remember when I started high school a year earlier than I was supposed to? How they let me skip eighth grade because I was academically advanced? I remember walking into the large building and not knowing anyone. I remember saying hello to the lamppost, to the hooded doors. I've never forgiven the birds that flew me to the door and left.

That year, when no one was looking, I stopped eating. That year, all food was undergrowth, something to hide from and hate. That year, food stalked me like the headlamps of a search party.

That was the year I began spending lunches in the library. I waited for my stomach to clench. I waited for you to forgive me. But you never did. This morning, I weighed myself and the numbers were ruinous again. The numbers that never seem low enough. I am at your mercy. At the mercy of your praise that never comes. I want you to be shaped like a teardrop, not a knife.

I read somewhere that eating disorders are about control. I read somewhere that victims of bullying are at increased risk of symptoms of anorexia and bulimia.

You look like you've gained weight, Father sometimes said to my sister when he still made sense. Father never said that to me. My own body was thinner, taller, more precise, and weighed one hundred forty-two years. I had fed it hawthorn berries and talons. Occasionally the talons punctured my stomach. Everything leaked out but desire.

I remember Mother often going on diets. One year, it was Shaklee's chocolate shake diet. Cardboard cans of brown powder lined the shelves. Another year, the brown rice diet, something she had learned from a Chinese family in California, who also told her to chew twenty times per bite. Another year, it was the red rice diet. Back to the brown rice diet. Then red. Still, Mother was slightly heavier and rounder than her other thinner, smaller Chinese friends.

At Mother's funeral, a bony Chinese man said, *Your mother was always a bit chubby. I was always worried about her health.* As if her weight had caused her lungs to fail. He didn't mean any harm, just as Father never meant any harm. But harm is rarely about intention. I remember all the times aunties would say to me, *You've lost weight.* Or, *You've gained weight. Stand up so we can see you better.*

A month before Mother died, she was so frail. She had lost all the weight of seventy-four years. I don't think she was finally happy. She looked small and beautiful in a baggy old dress with blue flowers that she could finally fit into. I was secretly happy that she would never have to worry about her body again. That the weight of caring for Father was gone, that the weight of her countries was gone, that she was finally the weight of light.

Great great grandmother

It's good that I can't see

Father: far right, back

your faces. If I could, I would

erase you with my words,

meaning writing has

Great grandfather left, Great uncle, right

Grandmother and Grandfather, father's side

something to do with love.

• *Father's family* •

中華民國人民出租用
內政部稅法民宅專
政股費民貴

Dear Teacher,

In the video online, you looked nothing like I remembered. Your hair all gray, glasses, and a full moustache. I remember you were tall, but in the video, you looked so much shorter. Most days, I can't hear people speaking, but I still hear your voice reading Hemingway: *It was now lunch time and they were all sitting under the double green fly of the dining tent pretending that nothing had happened. . .*

It must have been an English class in the large public high school I attended in West Bloomfield, Michigan. You stood at the front of the class in your tweed jacket and jeans, with your long brown bushy hair and beard. You read us entire books aloud with zest and at a remarkable speed, as you tried to convince us that literature meant something. I still have your handouts from that Hemingway module—"The Killers," "The Battler," "The End of Something." My notes in the margins on setting, characterization, theme, plot, climax, tone, point of view. The papers all yellowed like memory.

You loved to read books. You spent your entire day pacing with a kind of swagger, talking, one hand in your pocket. I was a silent Chinese American girl who never said a word in class, who went to the library at lunch.

I remember Amy, one of the popular girls, floating through the hallways with her football-star boyfriend, Jim. I remember how unconcerned they seemed, holding hands that always looked like grenades.

I remember the loud slamming of the lockers and how I tried not to bump into people for fear of being caught alive. I remember your voice, reading us short stories. *It isn't fun anymore,* from Hemingway's "The End of Something," as *Nick looked on at the moon, coming up over the hills.* I remember

Marjorie and how she didn't make a scene when Nick broke up with her. I, too, have never made a scene.

Years later, I wrote you an email telling you that I became a writer because of you, because of your class. I wrote that you probably didn't remember me. You wrote back saying that you did remember me, that you always knew there was something *burning beneath*. I didn't even care if you were lying. You were right. Poets live between a fire and a great fire.

Recently, in an interview for his radio show, Michael Silverblatt said: *The things you're talking about get covered up in the family. . . and one of the things about children's books is that it's very useful when language is provided to talk about the inner wordless experiences that we all have.*

Even though I couldn't see myself in Marjorie or Nick or Francis Macomber or Robert Wilson or even Hemingway, their emotions punctured through to me. At that point, literature curricula in the United States mostly consisted of white authors, white characters. But as I wrote *characterization* in the margins of "The Short Happy Life of Francis Macomber," I felt that we each had our own unique stories and that stories could teach us how to begin to unpack the *inner wordless experiences we all have.*

Recently I tried to send you another email, but it bounced back with no forwarding address. Your retirement article said that you had over 8,000 students. Maybe you don't want to hear from the 632nd student anymore. What could I possibly want you to say? Maybe I am like Marjorie, afloat in my own boat with the moonlight on it. The sound of me, rowing away on the water.

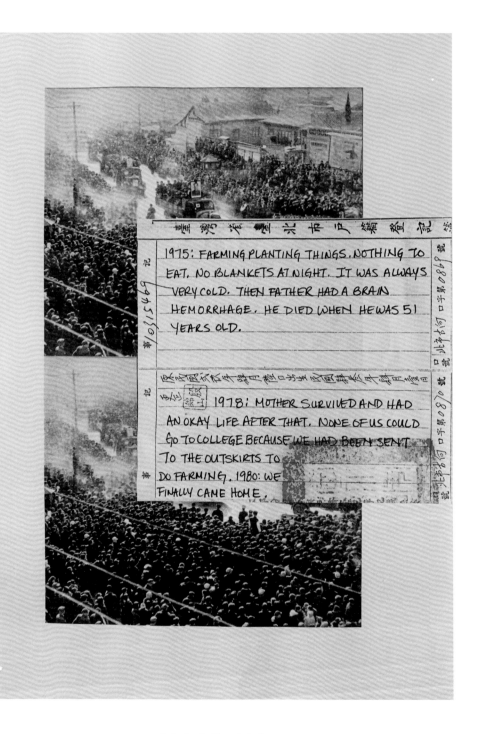

Mother's Cousin's letter

Dear L,

Somehow, I ended up at the party where you sat behind the stereo putting your cassette tapes in. You were the first Chinese American boy I had met outside of family friends. Like the trees in winter, we were all nearly dead. But you were from another city. I didn't know there were other cities until you came.

The room was filled with people. Strobe lights. Maybe a disco ball. When I shook your hand, I knew there was a horizon. And more than a past I could never find.

You had a girlfriend who was there. But I don't remember her. Memory works like this. You are astonished. You remember only what astonishes you.

Trauma can work the other way. Something is horrible. And then everything is amplified. The sound of the plane at that moment. The smell of the bomb. The small piece of lint in your pocket. The bell before death arrives. I wonder what my mother saw when she left China. What she held inside. When she died, I thought there had to be letters to me inside her body, but someone burned her body.

Dear L, you wrote me letters for years. We talked about music. Something was supposed to happen but I wasn't sure what. Now I see your letters as having a valve. You were eighteen. You wanted me to open the valve, but I wasn't sure how.

I hatched a plan to visit you. I planned to sleep over at Jane's house and then drive to see you. My hands held the wheel tightly as if I were driving desire. I learned that day that desire doesn't throb, it moves forward. I had a vague idea how to find your dorm. I had a vague idea how to drive on a freeway. I was sixteen, maybe seventeen. The day was supposed to be like the word *resplendent*.

By the time I found you, it was dusk. Not the muscular kind of dusk, but the kind that looks away when you look at it. You sat on a small dorm bed and I on the other across from you. I wonder whose bed I sat on that day and how he still doesn't know that he slept with my desire.

You had classes to study for. New friends to hang out with. The same girlfriend. The room smelled like dirty socks. Looking back, this was when I began to misunderstand desire. This was the beginning of wanting to put out the small fire that could never be put out.

We talked about nothing. I had a toothache that I thought covered my desire. I still depended on my mother to take me to the dentist. I yearned for the day I could take myself to the dentist. Soon. I knew. Soon. I now know my mother probably mourned no longer needing to take me to the dentist. Perspective creeps, like wisdom, but can feel sudden. As Mary Oliver wrote in her notebook, *Today I am altogether without ambition. Where did I get such wisdom?*[vii] When I finally found my way home in the red Ford Escort, my parents were waiting for me in the driveway. *Where were you?* my father demanded. He was a small man with a large head. I think at that point I was taller than he was. *At Jane's house,* I said, as I walked casually toward the garage. *No you weren't!* he shouted. Then he began kicking and hitting me.

That night, everything had a pewter tint. Family friends came over, and I remember a muffle of Chinese downstairs. I felt that something had been taken away, but it was something I never knew I had. I went to bed so heavy with that missing that, when I woke up, it was a different year.

Mother's Cousin: The government came
to our house and took everything,
burned everything. I fear if you
had stayed, what would have
happened to you. We had to burn all of
our family photos because your father
was wearing a kuomintang uniform in them.
I asked my mother why we didn't leave like
you and she just said that the people she
worked for told her not to go.

I used to hate red.

The color of meat and

Shame. Now I paint my

lips red so I don't disappear.

Dear Teacher,

The tall, handsome boy who was reading my poem aloud in front of the class had stopped cold, turned around, and begun whispering to you. The rooms in the windowless high school always seemed too bright, as if they knew they were about to lose to darkness.

You called me up to your desk. I hated getting up and walking around in class. I was unremarkable and strange. I was remarkably Chinese. I was so Chinese that I didn't know that I shouldn't have written a poem about contemplating suicide for a class assignment.

I was so Chinese that I didn't know that an American teacher might see this as a problem. At the same time, though, I had no idea what being Chinese meant. I had no idea what being American meant. I was here and nowhere. I could still hate something I didn't understand. I could still be something I didn't know.

You couldn't help me. I needed to be in a different country, where people looked like me, even a different state, like California. Where people didn't ignore me. Where people, when they did see me, didn't pull their eyes out thin and laugh. But that wasn't going to happen. And I couldn't see outside the funhouse mirror of my life.

The racist act is not always the most harmful. It's the surprise of it, the fraught waiting, each moment like a small trip wire. You never know when you might confront it, so to survive, you live your life in stillness, in self-perpetuated invisibility. And then there's the aftermath of shame.

Dear Teacher, you read us so many poems, so much Shakespeare, had us memorize so many poems, that I never became American, but I became a writer.

Because I could not stop for Death –
He kindly stopped for me –
The carriage held but just Ourselves –
And Immortality.

These words have passed through my brain almost daily. How you loved Dickinson. I remember your frilly old-fashioned powder blue blouses, tucked into tight pencil skirts, your gray hair, small wire spectacles, nylons, and little flats, how you pranced in front of the classroom reciting:

I'm Nobody! Who are you?
Are you — Nobody — too?
Then there's a pair of us!
Don't tell! they'd advertise—you know! . . .[viii]

I don't know how much of Dickinson or Shakespeare or Keats stuck in my teenage mind, but to learn from you that writing was a possibility, not as a career, but simply as a way to move into and out of pain, was the real gift.

I'm not sure if you are still alive and, if you are, you probably don't remember me, but that chasm between us was filled with poetry instead of misunderstanding. Instead of silence. When you shared poems with me, you were filling the space between us with language.

I didn't know what was happening at the time, but I see it now. The language of poetry reminded me to stay alive. It reminded me that, when it felt like I had nothing, I was nothing, I still had words. I could ride language as if on horseback, and it could take me anywhere, including more deeply into myself.

I don't remember what I told you when you called me up to the front of the classroom and whispered in my ear. I'm sure my face was expressionless and burning. But I remember how your hair curled at the bottom, as if shaped by a roller, how you smelled like perfume and joy. I still remember the way your eyes looked desperate and worried, their insistence that I step out of something. You weren't satisfied with my silence.

I remember nodding as if I was fine. I *was* fine. I had language. And it would be the one thing that would keep returning, like light. Language felt like wanting to drown but being able to experience drowning by standing on a pier.

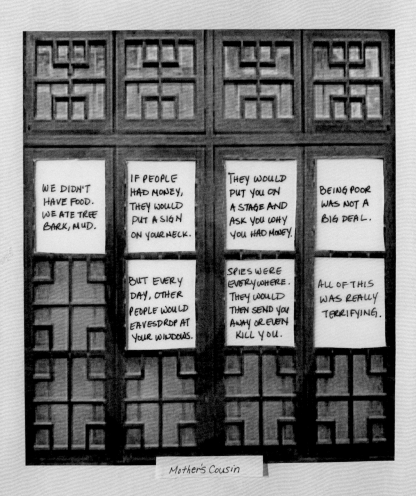

Mother's Cousin

Dear Mother,

Recently I found your marriage license. I know so many things now. I know you were twenty-four and Father was twenty-six. I know Father was a project engineer at General Motors, and you were a research assistant in the physics department at the University of Michigan. I know you went to the county to get married. I know your parents' names: Pao-Lan Jin and Gee-In Chang.

I wonder about your witnesses and where they are now. Wen-Jei Young and She-Zuan Zang. They lived at 2214 Yorktown Drive in Ann Arbor, Michigan. Were they roommates? Were they dating? I've never known if you can determine gender in a Chinese name. I never thought to ask before.

I wonder where the two county clerks are now—Luella M. Smith and Carol A. Miller. This language slips right off my tongue. I know these are both conventionally women's names. I know that Smith and Miller are common American names. I know the middle letters are middle initials.

I now know the year was 1966, three years before my sister would be born and four years before I would be born. I can't read the judge's name, but I think the judge was a man. I know his name is in cursive. I wonder what he thought when four Chinese people came into his court. I wonder if he felt a kind of prickling on his face. I wonder whether he was happy for you.

I imagine you, sweating under your nice dress. I imagine the dress was a pastel blue. I imagine the horizon that day bending toward the countries you left. I imagine you were relieved. That you felt wild. That you were scared.

I wonder why you never spoke of this day. I wonder how much of this day was about being practical. I wonder how much of this day was about love.

You had come to this country on your own. Who would marry you? Probably not an American. How would you find a Chinese man? How would you survive here by yourself? With no language. No money. Only secrets. You can't buy anything with secrets.

Father lived at 1021 Church Street in Ann Arbor. Google Maps brings up a little red house the color of a blush I might wipe on my face. I wonder how many Chinese people lived there. I wonder if he ever stood on the pretty porch. I wonder, when he came down the steps, if he turned right or left, I wonder if he picked that house because it was red.

You lived at 825 East University Street in Ann Arbor. Google Maps brings up a dilapidated yellow house with a gabled roof. According to Redfin, in 2016, the *entire building underwent wall-to-wall renovations*. I imagine them painting over your fingerprints.

I wonder why you never told me you lived in Ann Arbor, that you worked at the University of Michigan. Even when I went there myself, you never said a word. I wonder why you told me so little. Or maybe I wasn't listening because your past was unimportant, something to be forgotten.

I wonder whether memory is different for immigrants, for people who leave so much behind. Memory isn't something that blooms but something that bleeds internally, something to be stopped. Memory hides because it isn't useful. Not money, a car, a diploma, a job. I wonder if memory for you was a color.

When we say that something takes place, we imply that memory is associated with a physical location, as Paul Ricoeur states.[ix] But what happens when memory's place of origin disappears?

I imagine another kind of mother, an American mother, who might have walked me to 825 East University Street, arm in arm, finger pointing at the crow on the roof of the building. Telling me about Father, about her first kiss, about her crushes—secrets I could swallow.

Just two weeks ago, apartment #3 was for rent, the one on the second floor. I wonder what floor you lived on. Whether you had a nice view. If you had Chinese roommates. I wonder what you made for dinner each night. I wonder so hard, I can smell the rice cooker and hear the steam.

Google Maps tells me you lived two minutes from Father. I imagine Father visiting you, walking up Church Street, taking a left on Oakland Avenue, and then a right on East University. I imagine you walking down the stairs, no, flying down the stairs to open the door for him. Your heart in your throat by the time you reached the bottom. I imagine your cheeks tacked with desire.

I look on Google Maps to see if there's a ghost of you somewhere, of your leaping, of your dress lifting open. In this moment, your imagined happiness covers my grief like an eyelid.

Marriage License

WASHTENAW   COUNTY, MICHIGAN

State File No. **337**

Local File No. _____

To any person legally authorized to solemnize marriage in the State of Michigan,

Greeting:

Marriage must be solemnized within 30 days of date of issue _in the State of Michigan_
between

Fu-Shueng Chang	and	Jeng Jin
Full name of male		Full name of female
26		24
Age at last birthday		Age at last birthday
1021 Church Street		825 East University Street
Residence No. Street		Residence No. Street
Ann Arbor, Michigan		Ann Arbor, Michigan
City Zone No. State		City Zone No. State
Taipei, Taiwan, China		Peipin, China
Birthplace—city and state		Birthplace—city and state
Project Engineer of GMC		Research Assistant in Physics Department
Occupation		University of Occupation Michigan
None		None
Number of times previously married		Number of times previously married
Shih-Tou Chang		Pao-Lan Jin
Father's full name		Father's full name
Phon-Mei Lee		Gee-In Chang
Mother's maiden name		Mother's maiden name

_____, and whose
Maiden name (if a widow)

parent's or guardian's consent, in case she has not attained the age of eighteen years, has been filed in my office. An affidavit has been filed in this office, as provided by Public Act No. 128, Laws of 1887, as amended, by which it appears that said statements are true.

In witness whereof, I have signed and sealed these presents,

this ___21st___ day of ___March___, A. D. 19 ___66___

LUELLA M. SMITH

County Clerk

Carol A. Miller

Deputy County Clerk

L.S.

This marriage license VOID 30 days after date of issue.

Certificate of Marriage

Between Mr. ___Fu-Shueng Chang___ and M ___Jeng Jin___

I hereby certify that, in accordance with the above license, the persons herein mentioned were joined in marriage by me, at ___Ann Arbor___, county of ___Washtenaw___, MICHIGAN,

on the ___2nd___ day of ___April___, A. D. 19 ___66___, in the presence of

___Wen-Jei Yang___ of ___2214 Yorktown Dr. Ann Arbor, Michigan___ and
Full name Residence—city and state

___Shu-Jnan Gong___ of ___2214, Yorktown Dr. Ann Arbor, Michigan___
Full name Residence—city and state

as witnesses. _____ _____
Signature of magistrate or clergyman Official title

___Ann Arbor, Michigan___
Post office address

THIS DUPLICATE must be delivered by the person solemnizing marriage to one of the parties joined in marriage.

I've never seen mother

smile like this before.

It is the kind of smile

that only others can see.

• *Mother and Father* •

Dear C,

You call me all the time, as if I am a small bowl of water and you a bird. The problem is that the bowl of water is always empty.

Thank you, C, for caring for my father. Thank you for calling me every week. Yesterday you called, and I realized you hadn't been contacting me to give me reports, but to talk. I see now you call me to tell me about your suffering.

A few days before my mother died, she said: *I'm done. I don't care about him anymore. I'm too tired.*

She pressed the button and crossed the street when the blinking man was still red. In the intersection, six crows descended. She chose to die so she wouldn't have to care for Father anymore.

The last time we took Father out to eat was the last time he would ever go out to eat. When we paused in front of a golf course, I looked in the rearview mirror to see if he had noticed it. His head turned slightly to the right. When we stopped, he looked at the white carts moving, the small people pushing dimpled balls around with their sticks.

I wondered if Father had remembered his obsession with golf. How he had taped photos of golf swings all over his walls, how he had played almost every day for ten years, until his stroke.

As we passed the golf course, nothing in his expression changed. And I knew then that his brain had become skeined, like the fake spiderwebs we spread out on the bushes each Halloween. How we gather them, stretch them, attach them to a corner and pull and pull.

I'm sorry, C. I put Father on Seroquel today. My mother would have never done that. But my mother died. My mother would have never put him in memory care. But my mother died.

Some days, I want to tell everyone I meet that my mother died. Sometimes I do tell them, just to see who reacts. Most people don't. Most people probably wonder why I am still writing about my mother. I want to tell them that it is because my mother is still dead.

I don't blame anyone for not reacting, for some people still live in a bright room. *A bright hour,* as Emerson says. We often say night falls. I think the night rises. I think the bright falls.

I wonder what the hat

was trying to cover?

The others have flowers

on their dresses.

All of your flowers were

on the underside.

Eventhen, your stare was

slightly lower, looking

right beneath where

happiness begins.

• Mother (far right) •

Dear Teacher,

I stumbled into your poetry workshop even though I wasn't studying poetry. I was one of the few graduate students there. I remember you at the head of a long wooden table, presiding, as if your chair were a throne. The room was brown with wood everywhere. We were knights of poetry. Our plates were white sheets of paper filled with our own flesh. Your words were infinite. They were an entire country.

At the end of class, you wrote each student a note. Your note said my poetry had become *poems out of poetry* and that my poems had begun to *strike forward to the possibility. . .* You also wrote that you wished I had made my voice more present in class and that my *form of articulation was far from shy.* You told me to *call to talk about next semester.*

I'm sorry for never saying a word in your class the entire semester. I'm sorry that striking forward scared me, made me numb, stitched my mouth closed. But you gave me so many new words that I didn't know how to use yet.

One student was burning metal even then. Sometimes I would watch her mouth move, the way the air would take the shape of her words. Watching her speak was a kind of bereavement.

Each breath was so beautiful, there couldn't be anything but loss.

Fall Reading List For Victoria:

> Louise Glück: *Descending Figure*
> > *The House on Marshland*
> Wallace Stevens: *Collected Poems*

Sappho: *Every shred possible?*
Neruda: *Collected*
Vallejo: *Posthumous Collected (I think)*

does Plath fit in your life—*Collected*—and Lowell—*Selected*

I've never told you this, but Plath does fit into my life. I still read Louise Glück's poems. I have read all of Sappho. I have listened to podcasts on Neruda. I have read Wallace Stevens' *Collected*, but not every poem. Only Vallejo I still haven't read much, twenty-seven years later. I'm sorry. I will try to read more Vallejo.

In another note, you wrote: *I'm waiting for you to write shorter + shorter + denser + denser + louder + louder poems. I'm in <u>HONOR</u> of this machine.*

If you saw my poems today, I hope you could see that I heard you even though you couldn't hear me. I have tried to write shorter + shorter + denser + denser + louder + louder poems. They have become so loud that each night I fold them into origami cigarettes and smoke them so they'll blow away.

What I learned from you was to forget the sun, that the moon burned more, to cling to things that didn't seem to leave a trace, such as memory or silence or cruelty or beauty. I couldn't fully understand any of this then.

I wouldn't take another poetry class for a decade. But because of you, poetry kept on pricking me. Your voice stayed upstairs for years. I could hear it asking me questions I wasn't yet ready to answer. I now know there are no answers. You meant for me to listen to the questions and into the absence.

I'm sorry there was never a *till then*—. I'm sorry I never called you to talk about the next semester. I'm sorry I wasn't ready for all the conversations we never had. For never thanking you, for letting decades pass without another word.

My earliest memory is the time my mother scolded me in Chinese through a rearview mirror. *You have such a big mouth,* she said between tears and crying. *You can't say anything. Can't tell them anything.* I was five. I didn't know who *them* was. I didn't know what *anything* meant. All I could see were Mother's eyes in the rectangle. Even then, she didn't have a mouth.

Apparently, I had told my teacher that we had the same workbook at home. The teacher called my mother in and told her that she wasn't allowed to teach me on her own. Actually, I don't know exactly what the teacher told my mother. I was five. All I remember is my mother's tears and my empty stomach. The ketchup stain on the seat. The slaughterhouse in my throat.

It's only now that I think of how new my mother was to this country. How a comment from an American teacher could possibly make her scared. How she was just trying to help me do well.

My mother never talked to me about this incident again, and it's only after her death that I've started to think more about how she felt. Do you know that Salman Rushdie in *Shame* encapsulates this alienation so lushly: *It is the fate of migrants to be stripped of history, to stand naked amidst the scorn of strangers upon whom they see rich clothing, the brocades of continuity and the eyebrows of belonging.*[X]

On November 14, 2014, Ealy Elementary was demolished. When it happened, I thought about my mother and the promise I had given her. The promise never died with that building. There's still a brick inside my throat. I don't have roots, just the brick. The brick is silence. I know that I must bury the brick in order to speak, but how do you bury something that has no body?

Dear Teacher, the brilliant student in your class never stopped writing beautiful poems. Recently I watched a video of her reading in public and talking about one of *my* poems. To hear my words in her mouth, words that had come out of the quiet of that room was astonishing.

If you saw me today, you would know that I heard you. That I'm still trying to find words that can *strike forward to the possibility*—but I try not to grab them because you taught me that words are not meant to be owned. I marvel from the side at their madness. The striking is not academic. It wears a leather jacket on some days. It changes with weather. On rainy days, it is beautiful and has two-inch talons.

I still carry the brick around with me everywhere I go, but it is now outside of my throat. Sometimes I use it as a paper weight. Other times, it's so light that it feels like I no longer have it at all.

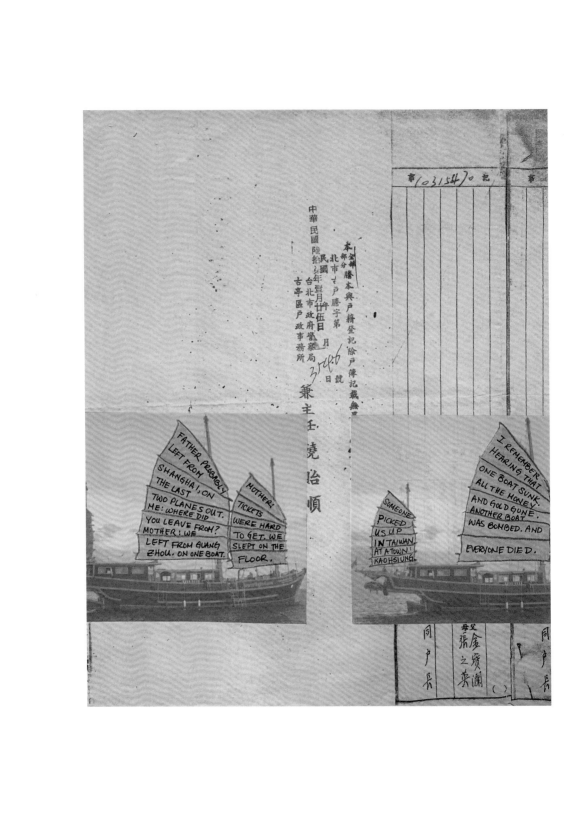

Dear T,

Remember the story you told me about your name, how it was your grandmother's maiden name? You were a tall, benevolent figure. Blue eyes. Skin as white as any woman from an English novel. I was twenty-four, you twenty-one. I thought you were so young, yet already you seemed to know so much more than I did.

I never shared an office with you. You always sat on the other side of the building, near all the partners. You had the perfect kind of education, one that I was familiar with, but in a different way. Private school. Princeton. You played squash. I learned from you that squash was something other than a gourd that came out of the ground.

I was lucky to be born in America. Lucky to have parents who couldn't drive home. Lucky not to know my relatives or countries. Lucky to know people like you. Lucky to be educated here, for the opportunities granted to me. Being so lucky also meant taking in knowledge from others, the way everything accepts the moon without question.

You told me that the partners admired you because of the way your mind turned around problems. I think it was also because of your lineages, the way you walked, your beauty. The partners, all men, could tell that you had never been exiled. The way they looked at you was terrifying. I hid my envy, so eventually it stacked up in my office and the woman who came in each night to vacuum stopped coming.

Do you remember the way you looked at my necklace and asked, *Is that real?* knowing it couldn't be. *I don't know,* I said, knowing it wasn't. I had bought it one night while watching QVC. *Diamoniques* is what the two beautiful white women called them, as if by buying this jewelry, I could be white, too, or have beautiful white all-knowing friends like them. Like you.

Well, it can't be real, you said. I lied. *I have no idea.* You insisted, *Well you would know if it was real.* Your mother had taught you. Your grandmother had taught your mother. At that moment, I wanted a grandmother too. I wanted one to teach me how to tell if a diamond was real or not.

Later that year, you showed me how to tell if a pearl was real. *You put it between your teeth,* you said. *If it's grainy, it's real. If it's slippery, it's fake.* Mine was slippery. *Fake,* you smiled.

When my mother died, I pried open all her red velvet clamshell containers. I remember mother dressing up to go to parties with her Chinese friends. I remember the clamshells and the jewelry she would put on. I remember thinking that the jewelry made her look like a queen. I don't remember when I began to think that the jewelry was gaudy. I don't remember when I began to listen to people like you, instead of Mother.

I put all the pearls between my teeth and gnawed. Most of them slipped off my teeth. None of the diamond rings fit. And I still couldn't tell if they were real or not. All I remember was that Mother was so anxious all the time that the entire house shook when she dreamed. My dreams are still filled with earthquakes.

All I knew was that Mother loved buying jewelry from QVC, and I remember hearing the women in the background pitch down blankets or blenders or shoes, as things piled up in her house, as she became sicker and sicker.

I also found some jade jewelry and jade animals. I've always avoided jade because it represented something Chinese. To assimilate meant that I rebuffed everything Chinese, especially jade, especially red.

I put a jade fish in my purse for good luck, the same fish my mother had once given me that I never took. I found a gold ring with three rubies in one of the boxes. Maybe they weren't real rubies. Maybe the ring wasn't really gold. Maybe it didn't matter. Maybe there is no real anything.

I slipped the ring on my fourth finger, but it was too big. I put it on my middle finger and haven't taken it off since. Throughout the day, I look at it often and marvel at its fakeness, that is both luminous and real.

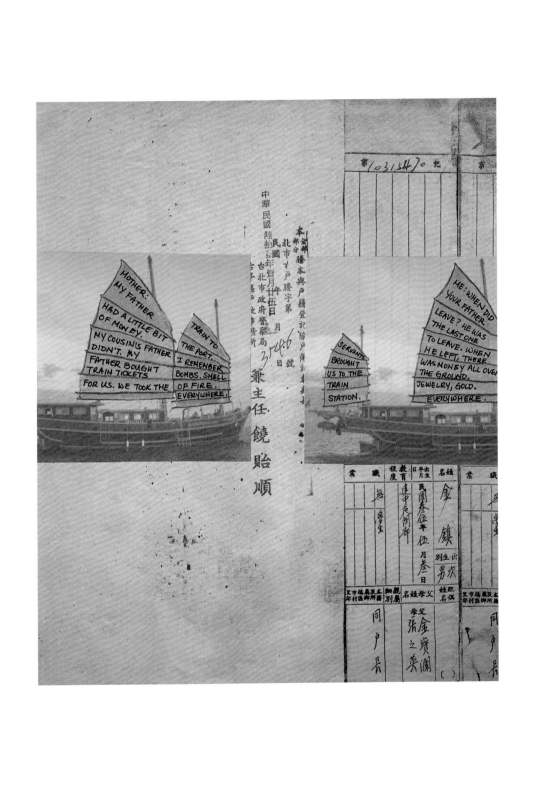

Dear G,

One more, c'mon, you said as you stood with your hands on your knees at the top of the football stadium. How many times did we run those stadium stairs? How many times did you reach the top before I did? By halfway up, my thighs felt like desks. Yet you and your long legs kept going. If I looked up, I saw stars and an elk running up a hill into the moon.

During the first week of business school, we played in the sports competition. You and I were paired together in a scramble golf tournament, meaning we each teed off but used the best ball for each hole. We mostly used yours, as you played golf in college. But once in a while my shorter, more consistent shots saved us from your wilder longer ones.

We won the tournament and shot three under par as a team. *I heard you and G killed the competition,* said Tom. *You're so athletic,* beamed Alex. Suddenly, I was the *cool athletic girl* in our class. *It was all G,* I said, wishing it weren't true.

I've always loved sports, the way the body pleats, the way limbs transform into instruments. My mother used to drop me and my sister off at the YMCA, telling us to swim fifty laps freestyle or fifty laps breaststroke, and then she'd pick us up hours later. She was my first personal trainer. I was stronger, bigger, and faster than my sister, and occasionally she would succumb to racing me if I begged hard enough.

I now wonder what my mother was doing while we were swimming. I wonder if she had a secret life. If she was smoking. If she had a lover. If she was visiting her favorite bakery with the seven layer cake.

My mother also introduced us to tennis. *You're pretty good,* said the coaches. *But you have to be more aggressive,* they would often add. Other athletic kids competed while I dabbled. No one I knew talked about competitions or teams or leagues. No one I knew played sports very seriously.

In high school, I envied the volleyball girls and their glossy, matching white jackets and then the tennis girls, with their short white skirts pleated like wings. I had never heard of JV or varsity. I didn't know how one might join a sports team. But I couldn't get those jackets out of my mind.

When I saw posters for tryouts, I asked my mother if I could try. *You can, but it's a waste of time,* she said. Tryouts, unbeknownst to me, weren't for learning how to play volleyball. You were supposed to have already been playing for years. My mother didn't see the value of sports beyond general fitness. Looking back, I think this was because she didn't grow up in a culture where sports dominated.

The ball was harder than I had thought. The ground was harder than I had thought. The girls were harder than I had thought. My heart, though, was just as soft as I had thought.

My mother drove me back and forth to tryouts. She never said much. Silence was her second language. Her looks throbbed more than the bruises on my forearms.

When the coach told me I didn't make the team and that I could be a manager, without thinking, to save face, I told him I would do it. I wanted that glossy white jacket. I also yearned to be a part of something that wasn't Chinese. I never did get the jacket, though. Those were for the players only.

I stood on the sidelines for a season with a clipboard and watched the powerful, mostly tall, large white girls easily pound a small soft ball that had seemed so large and firm to me. I watched my team members cheer and tried to copy them. Cheering and shouting in public felt like a new language. When they stood up, I stood up. When they sat down, I sat down. I kept records of kills and other things. I learned quickly.

After that year, I gave up on volleyball. As a senior, I tried out for the varsity tennis team. For a week, I hit balls with the other girls as the coaches watched us. I made the team as a doubles player. My partner and I weren't very good. We were the last string, the alternates. We would play the matches but our results rarely counted.

I didn't care. I had a white skirt, the collared shirt, the sweatshirt with my name in caps on the back. I got to be in my first—and last—team photo.

Once at a tournament, all the players who usually won, hadn't. Suddenly, we, the last to play because a few players were sick, would determine the entire team's results. I recall nothing of that match except the feeling of burning away and the team staring through the fence until their faces became diamonds.

If my doubt smelled like anything, it smelled like sandalwood. Before every shot, my body asked my brain what it wanted to do, but the brain had to ask the heart that had hidden itself near my ankles.

We lost. Our only match that mattered. Shame never has a loud clang. The worst part of shame is how silent it is.

That year, I didn't attend the year-end banquet. I wish my parents had encouraged me to go or that I had enough courage to convince myself, if only to show the value of teamwork and overcoming my own shame.

Someone told me that during the banquet, the coach said: *V is a good player. She's the only player who made the varsity team as a senior. She would have been even better if she had started earlier.*

With our own children, I vowed to have them *start earlier*. AYSO soccer. Basketball. Softball. We even coached some of these teams. *I don't like soccer*, one child said. She went entire seasons without going toward the ball, instead running parallel with the other kids, back and forth. If the ball came to her, she kicked it away so the other kids would swarm in another direction.

Do you want to try volleyball? I asked this year. *I hate volleyball*, one child said. *All those girls play volleyball*. I thought back to the girls on the volleyball team at my high school. Who exactly were they? And how did they become those girls?

We tried so many individual sports. Tennis, swimming, golf. Our children did these things with less complaining but with a similar lack of enthusiasm. One still swims, but dislikes competition.

A therapist told me that I should have my children choose a team sport, that it's essential to their development. When I told the children this while driving, I looked in the rearview mirror, only to see both of them crying.

I used to think that *those girls* meant white girls. But maybe it's also about disposition, readiness, aggressiveness. Maybe to not be *those girls* is, in our case, about fear of competition, about fear of being ashamed. Shame.

Maybe genetics are more fluid than I had imagined. Maybe we inherit generations of shame. Of trauma. Of silence. Even of joy. Recently, I began learning of *transgenerational trauma* and the *conspiracy of silence*, although I have mixed feelings about the word *conspiracy*, its implication of intent.

Growing up, I had never thought much about whether my parents experienced trauma or that my parents', particularly my mother's trauma impacted me. She was her own person. Her experiences didn't have anything to do with my experiences. Research and reflection now show otherwise. That while my parents may have maintained silence as a form of survival, silence had a heartbeat, grew up, and became the third sibling.

I've since read that children of immigrant parents simply don't have the experience or context with which to understand their parents' trauma, so the trauma continues onto the next generation in a different form. This new trauma departs from the old trauma's already unstable relationship to memory.

Back in that old high school gym, the volleyball went low. *Dive,* the coach yelled. I tried to dive, but right before my body hit the ground, fear came from my body, as if something from my history was telling me not to do it, not to dive. When I had to cheer for my teammates, my voice felt still-birthed.

I ignored the therapist in the end. Maybe turning my children into Americans wasn't going to be as easy as I had thought. Maybe by *American,* I really mean *white*. Maybe my children are already American, but a different kind of American. Maybe my children don't need to be white, especially growing up in a diverse state such as California. And maybe my children aren't really themselves. They're thousands of years of other people. Cultures. My trauma. Mother's trauma. Father's trauma. Their silence. Passed down through me.

This weekend, our twelve-year-old competed in her first (and probably last) track meet. Her friends were participating, so she had asked to, as well. She had never asked to do any sport before. Not soccer. Not softball. Not volleyball. Not tennis.

I was traveling, but I watched the video of her running the 4x100 and the 100-meter. She wasn't fast and wasn't slow, and she wore loose, ill-fitting clothes, but it was a wonder, beautiful, like watching a hummingbird resting on a branch, escaping itself and its history for a moment that seemed to last generations.

Dear Teacher,

I remember you sitting at the head of our small rectangular table in a class-room where I, along with a motley group of mostly older women, decided to take a writing class. Some of us were new to poetry, but many of us were trying to find a way back to poetry as adults.

Poetry was still thousands of miles away though. Despite being in my thir-ties, I was still learning how to pronounce my own name. Do you know that Li-Young Lee said that *a sentence is a unit of identity. . . . A line, too, is an instance of identity?*[xi] For me, writing felt like an act of identity-making. Each word, a clavicle, a femur, each sentence, an organ.

I still remember how excited you seemed the day you told us that your book would be published. At that very moment, I decided that I, too, wanted to publish a book, just one book of poems in my life. If someone who looked like me could publish a book of poems, then maybe I could do the same. How little I knew at the time, that both writing and publishing could be relentlessly unforgiving.

During the break, as you lay the little workshop papers down on the ground, got on your hands and knees to sort them, I said, *Congratulations on your new book!* You leaned and bent, white papers in small stacks staring up at me like faces. *Thanks!* you said. After that, a wind kept blowing in my body. Even when I shut my mouth, the wind kept leaking in.

I still remember the joys of my first book. It's true, except in the rarest of circumstances, a first book most likely won't change one's life in immedi-ate, external ways. But I know my first book changed me. I never stopped wanting after that. Not only books, but to be surprised again and again by the possible collusions of language. And the more I read, the more I realized how hard writing well really was. The more I read, the better I wanted to write.

Each book isn't just a book, but a period of a life, a period of learning how to write. Each book has its own hair color, its own glasses, its own favorite mug, its own computer, its own shirt and pants, its own tears.

Sometimes I think that writers are too self-absorbed. I often think about what Sylvia Plath wrote: *I think writers are the most narcissistic people. Well, I mustn't say this, I like many of them, a great many of my friends are writers.*[xii] I think writing requires one's full attention, but for me, that attention and obsession is toward language. As I write, more and more of my cells are replaced by language. When they burn a writer's body, the smoke will be shaped like letters.

Sometimes writing can feel like digging holes, planting and replanting things that might never turn into anything. My eyes point down when I'm planting, but the breath of something else is always in my ears. Sometimes that breath is mortality. Other times, that breath is history. Sometimes memory. Sometimes the moon. Oftentimes, silence.

Plath said something like this too: *I think that personal experience is very important, but certainly it shouldn't be a kind of shut-box and mirror looking, narcissistic experience. I believe it should be relevant, and relevant to the larger things.*[xiii]

Dear Teacher, everything you taught me, I took with me. You gave me a flashlight and pointed me to a hole in the ground. But like the best teachers, you didn't tell me what I'd find there. I kept the flashlight and have been wandering in caverns since then. I haven't seen the sun since we met. I live on drips of moisture from the earth. I eat leftover snacks from the pockets of dead writers.

Dear Teacher, you had us read so much in such a short period of time. I still remember how we talked about Jeanette Winterson in your class. And how Winterson wrote that *the most powerful written work often masquerades as autobiography. That it offers itself as raw when in fact it is sophisticated. That it presents itself as a kind of diary when really it is an oration.* I love when Winterson says that *the best work speaks intimately to you even though it has been consciously made to speak intimately to thousands of others.*[xiv]

Now I admire writers who write with an intimate intensity but also a generous capaciousness. I enjoy reading work that expands while it contracts. Writing made by an instrument with a microscope on one end and a telescope on the other, leaving some powder on the page in the form of language.

A5891148

戶號 北市城國戶字第 167 號　　　　　　戶 共同生活戶：別戶

事A20154828記—○　　事A10156777記—4　　行政區劃及住址

MOTHER: EVERYONE WAS IN A WAREHOUSE. WE HAD TO WAIT. THEY CALLED US BECAUSE OUR BOAT WAS READY. WE SLEPT ON THE FLOOR AND WE PUT OUR LUGGAGE ON THE SIDE. MY GRANDMOTHER BROUGHT RICE AND VEGETABLES, PLATES, AND BOWLS. WE ONLY WAITED A FEW DAYS IN THE WAREHOUSE. TAIWAN DIDN'T HAVE ANY TYPHOONS SO THE WEATHER WAS NICE.

I DON'T KNOW HOW MANY DAYS WE WERE ON THE BOAT. I REMEMBER IT WAS AUGUST 1949. OUR ESCAPE LUCK WAS VERY GOOD. THERE WERE SO MANY PEOPLE IN CHINA AND NOT MANY OF US WERE ABLE TO LEAVE AND MAKE IT TO TAIWAN. WE WERE VERY VERY LUCKY.

中山　明勝一　通河

區　里　鄰　部街路門牌

街路　街路　街路　街路　路段
段　段　段　段　十八

街巷　街巷　街巷　街巷　57-1
號　號　號　號

部份（教育程度職業）複查（借供參考用）印

口號 北市城國口字第0597號　　口號 北市城即字第0596號

妻　　　　　　戶長　　　　全戶助態記事　　戶長變更記事

職業　教育程度　出生年月日　姓名　　職業　教育程度　出生年月日　姓名

無　國校畢業　民國卅五年壹月柒日　李達妹　　無　認字　民前江年拾貳月貳日　張石頭

女　出生別　　　　　　　　男次　出生別

職業　家庭管理

父母姓名　父 李水玉　母 張網妹　　　配偶姓名 李達妹　　父 張網　母 張林賴心

本籍及住所　同戶長　　　本籍及住所 台北市

TWO MILLION PEOPLE FOLLOWED THE KMT TO TAIWAN BETWEEN 1945-1949.

Dear Daughters,

One summer I interned at a large company that made chemicals into different sweet shapes of cartoon characters, called them fruit snacks, and told parents they were healthy. I had beaten out many people for the job because I said things they wanted to hear. Saying things others want to hear is easy for an immigrant's child because, for an immigrant's child, language is theater. We are always performing.

That summer, I left behind a boyfriend and packed a few suitcases to make my way to a new city. That boyfriend liked telling stories so that others loved him more. In this way, we were a perfect match. His favorite one was about his basketball team making it to the NCAA finals. That boyfriend glowed like only the wounded could. He was always moving. He was a forward. In hindsight, I dated him because he seemed to be everything I wanted to be. White, athletic, popular.

I found a nice apartment but felt unhoused. I rented a small car but felt like I was standing still. I tried to inherit the meadows but the meadows were fenced in. I remember an older man on the project team who said impatiently, *Just make the decision and stop asking us what we think.* I had chalk in my throat most days. Back then, I thought other people made decisions, that other people led teams.

Once when my boyfriend came to visit, we watched *The Phantom of the Opera.* He fell asleep a few times. I thought about what new chemicals we could make out of his breathing the next day. In my dream that night, I was wearing the Phantom's white mask.

My hands tapped on spreadsheets that calculated how many bags of snacks we could sell. I was supposed to put small numbers into rectangular boxes.

Instead, I sorted clouds. Averaged countries. Tried to divide loneliness. Sometimes at night, with a persistent moon, I could see the numbers beneath my skin.

I followed the other interns to happy hours, to meetings, but everything remained interior. I couldn't seem to get in sync with a country. I couldn't figure out if the country was where I buried my memories, or the ground that would bury me.

I felt as if I were staring at a painting that had more dimensions but I couldn't get inside. A co-worker was moving one weekend and I offered to help her because I thought that's what an American would do. I shook her hand so hard that I couldn't uncurl my hand for days.

Dearest Daughters, in your life, you will sometimes be the glove and sometimes the hand. But on some cold nights, you won't be able to see your hands at all. On some nights, you might feel like the last person who shook your hand took your hand with them.

On some nights, you will have a camera around your neck, unwanted, which is also my camera which is also your grandmother's camera and your great-great-great-grandmother's camera. You can't escape seeing with our eyes. But you also won't be able to see us.

Daughters, there will be some days when everyone around you looks like an executioner. There will be times when everyone sounds like you, but no one looks like you. There will be other times when everyone looks like you but no one sounds like you. It's okay, though. Those without history are difficult to harm. Because we are always moving.

That summer, I used up all the right words to get the job, but then I had no words left. That summer would be the ending and the beginning. The nice man who gave me the job later asked me about my summer experience. I told him that the job and the city weren't a good fit. What I should have said was, *I don't know how to interact with white people.* That *spending time in the Midwest felt like a step back into an old house that I thought had long fallen off the cliff.* I was sorry he hired me based on my words. Because under those 643 words were masses of flies.

It took me a long time to find my people: writers, creatives, and artists. My people didn't sit in cubicles and calculate sales forecasts for fruit snacks. It took me a long time to know my people existed, and even longer for me to seek them out.

Daughters, I have felt incomplete for most of my life. Please don't follow me. What I worry most is that you have already started following me. That you are from me. You both have my freckles. What else have I passed on?

Then through the door, I hear you playing a game on the computer with a friend. I listen to your perfect English and am bewildered by it, the beauty of the words, the precision of each pause, the curve of each idiom. Then I hear you laughing so loudly that the door shakes a little. And I put my head in my hands and weep.

Once you had to stand behind

Your grandmother who left a

Country, each of your feet

lifted off the land onto the

boat like nightingales.

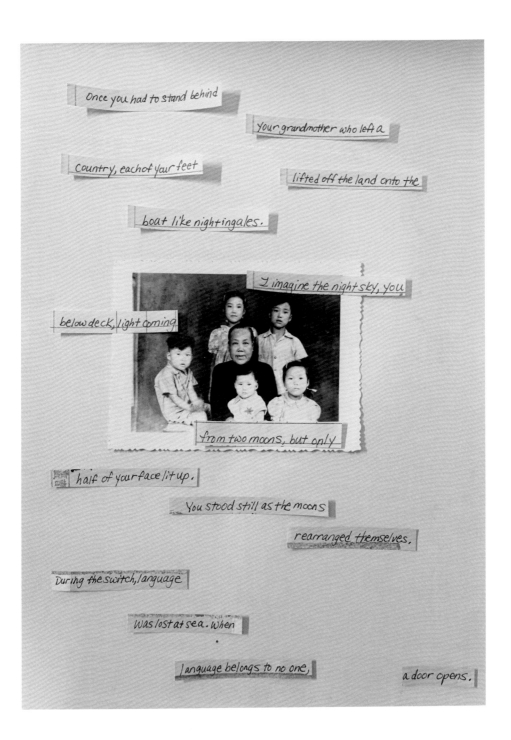

I imagine the night sky, you

below deck, light coming

from two moons, but only

half of your face lit up.

You stood still as the moons

rearranged themselves.

During the switch, language

Was lost at sea. When

Language belongs to no one,

a door opens.

· *Maternal Great-Grandmother (middle), Mother (center top)* ·

Dear Teacher,

You were the most rigorous teacher I've ever had. I imagine this is something you've heard before. At the time, your intelligence seemed like an outpost, perhaps in a different century. Have you ever noticed that *century* and *country* share all the same letters but one?

Not being an English major or having native English-speaking parents, I was challenged by your words, your letters. I read and reread, underlined, circled, double underlined, starred, put question marks next to them. Your words seemed so much older than mine. So much bigger than mine. Could this be possible? Could the same words you use and I use be that different?

Once you told me that sometimes I was in danger of outsmarting my poems, that sometimes my poems were written to illustrate an understanding I already had.

Do you know that Susan Sontag said something similar? *I think I am ready to learn to write. Think with words, not with ideas.*

You might know that Gertrude Stein said the same thing:

> You will write if you will write without thinking of the result in terms of a result, but think of the writing in terms of discovery, which is to say that creation must take place between the pen and the paper, not before in thought or afterwards in a recasting.[XV]

And Louise Glück talks about how writing is the act of learning to know:

At the heart of that work will be a question, a problem. And we will feel, as we read, a sense that the poet was not wed to any one outcome. The poems themselves are like experiments, which the reader is freely invited to recreate in his own mind. Those poets who claustrophobically oversee or bully or dictate response prematurely advertise the deficiencies of the chosen particulars, as though without strenuous guidance the reader might not reach an intended conclusion.[xvi]

Dear Teacher, Susan, Gertrude, and Louise, what you were saying to me in beautiful language was that I shaped and molded my poems into a meaning I already possessed. That my poems lacked discovery and wildness. The house was already built, and I took your hand and led you through the finished rooms where we marveled at the chandeliers which were preconceived thought.

I like the idea of the writing staying slightly ahead of thought. The way the moon always seems to be chasing a whale.

Later you told me to try and start each poem at a particular moment and pursue it as a path of discovery. I think you meant that I took all the power away from the poem because I thought words were thinking. Dear Teacher, I don't think I was able to find that path of discovery in the time I worked with you, but I promise you that I tried. And I am still trying.

I now think words are light. How they illuminate the small beak of a lark isn't up to the writer. It's up to the lark and the light. A writer is just a guest, the birder.

In one of my papers, you marked my misplaced modifiers, ambiguous pro-nouns, inaccurate punctuation, and split infinitives. Dear Teacher, you were the first teacher to uncover my grammatical errors. Until then, I had no idea.

How slanted my words may have seemed to you, each misplaced modifier, a hot poker in your eye.

After Father had a stroke, I packed up his books. Many of the books had markings on each page in red pen, some many more than others. Father had circled words he didn't know and written their definitions in the margins in Chinese. His circles were jagged, as if zigzagging a circle might somehow will words into meaning.

Sometimes I wonder how much grammar my parents didn't pass on to me. On the other hand, I can speak another language, Mandarin, decently. I wonder what it would have been like to grow up in a family where everyone spoke the same language. The only language we had wholly in common was silence. Growing up, I held a tin can to my ear and the string crossed oceans.

I kept one of Father's books, *The Kite Runner* by Khaled Hosseini. I read it and paused at the words Father didn't know. *Pelted*, circled in red, then a light red line to the margin and tiny Chinese characters I couldn't read. *Appendage, intricate, wrought-iron, tapestry* . . . And then all the circled phrases.

The first time I had read *The Kite Runner*, I raced through it because the narrative moved so quickly and the writing seemed simple in diction, syntax, and vocabulary. This time I got to see how slowly Father read the book. I always thought he knew everything.

After a while, coming upon a circled word sparked a curiosity: *What word didn't Father know?* Occasionally the words in the margin were in English. I became enamored with how the mind folds one language into another. Not what is lost, but what is gained.

Recently we took Father out to eat at a local noodle shop. With his right hand, he picked up his chopsticks, grabbed some noodles, and with his left hand, picked up a napkin. Father proceeded to transfer the noodles into the napkin. I wondered about this long after watching him. He never ate anything in the end.

As we left, the other mostly Chinese people in the restaurant stared at him as he shuffled to the door, hair too long, pants partially unbuttoned. I became aware that I had gotten used to his odd appearance and behavior.

As I pulled his sweatshirt forward, I thought, *Father can no longer read*. All that work circling English words in all those books over all those decades, gone. That was the last time we took him out to eat.

Dear Teacher, twenty years ago, I asked you if a writer needs to suffer. I wasn't yet convinced that I had suffered enough compared to other writers that I knew. Mother hadn't committed suicide. Father hadn't abandoned me. Sister didn't die in a car crash. Father didn't beat me (unless I truly deserved it).

You told me that suffering can deepen and expand a poet's work. And that sometimes suffering can put so much pressure on a person that they have no choice but to become a poet. You told me that suffering is one's fate and that regardless of whether the fates have distributed suffering to me, if I see the world around me, care about and for other people, face the setbacks of the world, read with hunger, get older, encounter illness, and if life is not lost on me—and if, all the while, I learn how to write better and to pay attention better—maybe, just maybe, I would be able to write better poems.

Dear Teacher, I hope I have found ways to deepen and enlarge my writing. I have tried to look closely at the world around me. I have cared about and deeply for other people. I try and read with real hunger, have had setbacks, have aged, and have encountered illness and death. I hope life has not been lost on me. And I hope my grammar has improved in the process.

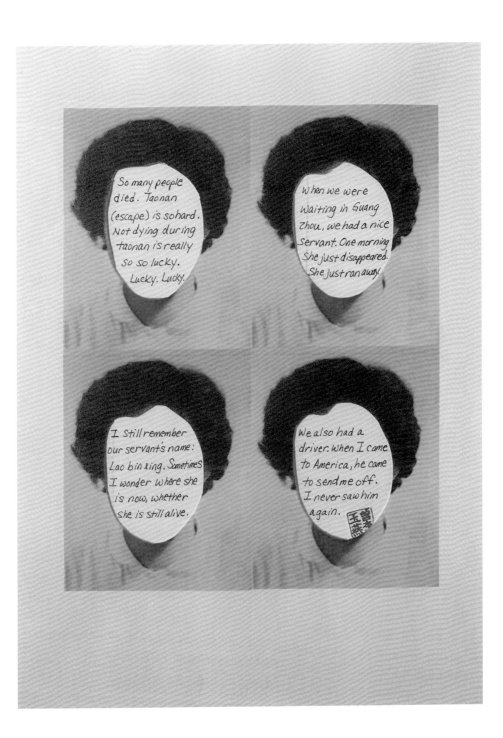

• Mother •

Dear Sister,

When did we start grieving the world separately? Do you remember our small Pooh bears? Each six inches tall, from Sears. How Father used to bring them home after traveling, and then we had seven.

Each had thin fur, black vinyl eyes and a nose, a string for a mouth, two pink ears, a red shirt. Each was packed with sawdust, which made them firm, and as the label said, *for decoration only.*

I named each based on how they looked and I called them the Seven Links. One day, they began to talk, not to each other, but to you. Each one spoke in a slightly different voice. Fatty spoke the most. Fatty with the mischievous personality, wild and free, always joking in a dark cold house.

If Fatty was me, then Skinny was you. Lighter-skinned, shorter, one eye missing, one ear missing. Smarter. Awkward. Quiet. Moody. Secretive. Skinny smelled like bananas. Once Skinny started talking, all the bears did. And we rarely spoke in human voices again.

Want to play? asked Fatty. *No,* you replied. I tried again with a different bear. *I'm going to study, I'm so smart,* said Skinny. Still no response. *You know, I went to Harvard,* said Skinny. You laughed, looked up from your book, *I didn't know that. What did you get on your SATs?* I picked up Petuie, the athlete of the group. *He got a full score.* You started laughing and put the book down. *Oh really?*

Once you got tired of my antics, you picked up your book. Snow tapped lightly at the window and the house began to fill back up with silence.

Once I threw Skinny against the wall so hard that he ruptured a bit. I think I was throwing you against the wall. I was throwing myself against the wall, the cut-out space between American and Chinese life. The cut-out space between you and me. Between our parents and us.

What I didn't know at the time was that that space would never fully disappear. It could not be acted through. The space was my life, a place of mourning. This would be the place I would write into and from within.

If you look at Fatty today, he is dark brown, almost black, with stains all over his face and body. He is soft, having lost half of his sawdust. His ear and nose are missing. He has two small bells I sewed to his feet. As if I were choosing joy. As if joy could be chosen.

Fatty now sits in a shoe box labeled *Fatty's House,* made by one of my children. Another child made a small pillow and bed for Fatty. Pruny shares the house with Fatty. My children know not to touch the box too often.

Skinny and Petuie were staying at your real house, the house on a busy road. You called me recently, crying, something that had never happened before. Since then, I have heard you cry one more time, when Mother died.

Someone had broken into your house and emptied out all the drawers. Skinny was in one of the drawers. *You had put Skinny in a drawer so your kids wouldn't touch him,* you said. I listened to you cry. The cruelest thing someone can do is to empty a drawer. Whoever stole Skinny took our childhood away.

When Father entered the ER for his stroke, brain bleeds, or falls, the hospital would sometimes put a stuffed bear on his bed. Father never seemed to notice the bears. But I took each of them with me.

When Mother was dying, I bought one daughter an overpriced stuffed elephant from the hospital gift shop. The elephant had a sack of flax seeds soaked in lavender that could be taken out, microwaved, and put back in. The elephant would then emit lavender.

Four years later, the elephant still sits on that daughter's bed, along with the tens of other stuffed animals currently in favor. Her body now the length of the twin bed. *Do you remember the lavender inside?* I asked her one day. *Yes,* she said. I asked, *Why don't you microwave it anymore?* She replied, *Because the scent has faded.*

Skinny is gone. Our mother is gone. Our father has faded. All our children are nearly grown and soon to fade away. We are still here, though. You and I, extending silence.

I'm thinking about how Mary Ruefle writes that *the moon was the first poem, an entity complete in itself, recognizable at a glance, one that played upon the emotions so strongly that the context of time and place hardly seemed to matter.*[xvii] Dear Sister, we are the moon.

Our childhood was the moon—entire, bare, silent, and overflowing. Each night, I do the only thing I know how to do—I climb back into it.

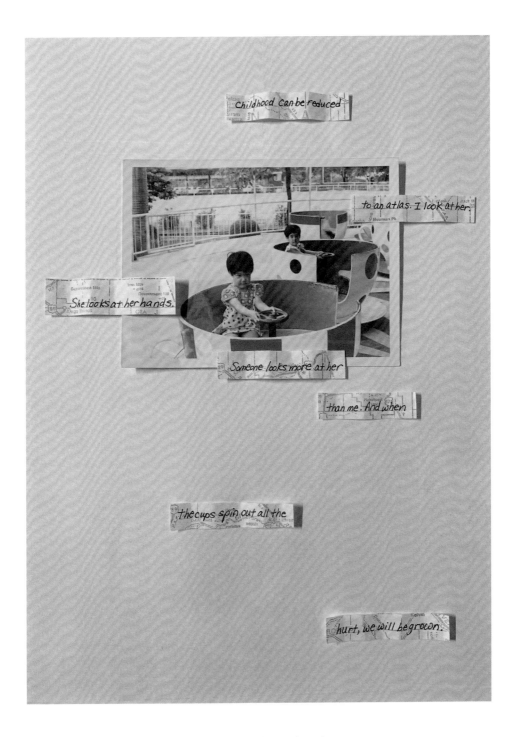

Childhood can be reduced

to an atlas. I look at her.

She looks at her hands.

Someone looks more at her

than me. And when

the cups spin out all the

hurt, we will be grown.

• Sister (front), me (back) •

Mother: I still remember that on the train, there was a girl who had a little brother and a little sister. Their parents were gone and they had no money. Every day, they ate chao suan tsai [pickled cabbage], no meat. Me: How old were they? Mother: She was maybe 18 and the others were smaller. Me: where did you get your food? Mother: on the side of the road, very cheap food. The girl came to visit us in Taiwan and then we never saw them again. Me: where were their parents? Mother: I don't know. Disappeared. No one knows. I still remember a woman holding a small child's hand to get on the boat and then she realized it wasn't her child. Me: what did she do? Mother: Brought her on the boat. There are too many stories like this. We were lucky. Lucky.

華民國政府專用章

中華民國政府專用章

內政部總務司印

Dear Teacher,

I shut my eyes as I waited for the woman in the pink uniform. *Wait here,* she said. The woman had said her usual speech, *I can't tell you what I see or don't see.* I had wondered how many ultrasounds she had already done just that hour.

Another woman wearing a white coat came into the room with the pink woman to her side. *It looks like you had some bleeding behind the placenta. And the bleeding may have affected your pregnancy . . .*

We couldn't locate a heartbeat.

More silence.

I'm sorry.

They left and I dressed, tucking darkness back under my clothes. When I saw people near the elevator, I turned the other way into the stairwell. Once alone, my body began to shake as I walked down into the earth.

It turned out he was a boy. He had an extra chromosome.

When you were my teacher, you had an unexpected illness. I never told you that I was upset that you hadn't sent feedback on my work when you had promised. I never told you that my greed had a heartbeat. That I equated a teacher's attention with my ability to become a better writer. I thought teachers could fix me. Could make me overheard.

At that time, something rang so loudly in my ears that I couldn't hear anything. I was in my thirties, still fascinated with myself. Much later, when I could finally hear, I heard that you may have had a miscarriage.

I think that when I learned about the miscarriage, it didn't upset me enough. I think I was too busy trying to find myself to be troubled by the loss of others. What I didn't understand at the time was that to find myself, I had to lose. To get lost. And that to become a better writer, I had to lose the self to the language.

I have often wondered how to teach my own children empathy. They say *I feel bad* in response to other people's pain often enough that I don't worry, but then I think back to myself and worry.

When I finally made it to college, my mother often drove the hour to visit me when I hadn't asked her to. Each time she brought a small tupperware container of food with a small stack of rice on the bottom, topped with braised tofu, diced pork, and dark green vegetables that gripped the side of the container like a country.

Now I imagine all the times she must have sliced extra meat and tofu to save a container for me. All the times she had rung the button in front of Betsy Barbour, the all-girls dorm at the University of Michigan. All the times I went downstairs, and she stood there a few steps below me and handed me the containers. All the times I took the containers without any words. My mother did so much for me. What I returned to her were empty containers.

The problem with silence is that you can't undo it. In that way, it's like death. Small silences toward my mother accumulated over the years. Now they return as a stack of grief.

Dear Teacher, I think often about your dead baby and my dead baby. My hospital wristband, the one that simply says *baby boy*, still sits inside my wallet like a tombstone. I imagine all the dead babies together somewhere on a large playground, swinging and sliding. And for a moment, I forget to grieve.

I had another doctor check just in case, hoping that it was a mistake. But the baby was still dead. Small black dots for eyes, paddles for hands. When the machine automatically printed out a picture of the baby, the doctor silently ripped it off and stuffed it in his pocket.

I paid a twenty-dollar copay to see a picture of my dead baby on a screen. On my way out, the doctor told me about his new Botox business and to come back soon. He would give me a discount.

Dear Teacher, I'm sorry for not having empathy or understanding until years later. My lack of empathy was a failure of imagination. And this failure showed up in my writing. My writing always had a layer of skin stitched over it.

In the years before Mother died, I drove hundreds of miles to the best Chinese restaurants in the area to bring her braised tofu and pork, vegetables, and dumplings. I liked watching her hunch over and comb the food with her chopsticks, shoveling in something not quite like joy, but familiarity, home, a country. I now think that mother wasn't just eating food. She was eating her memories, which were also my memories.

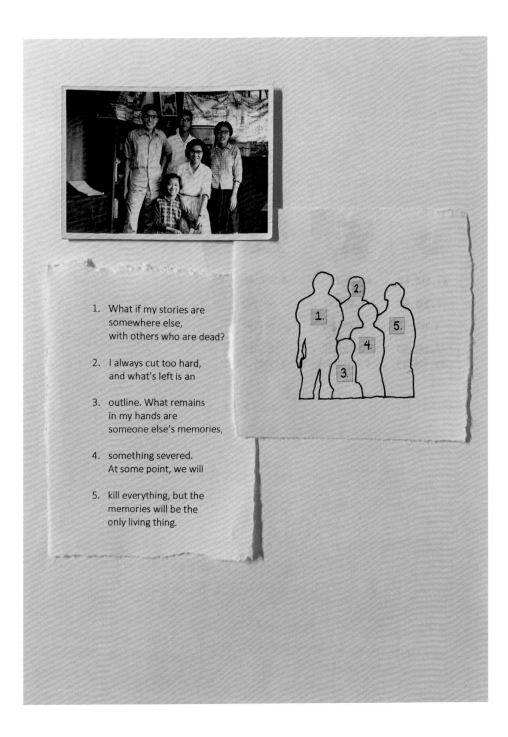

1. What if my stories are
   somewhere else,
   with others who are dead?

2. I always cut too hard,
   and what's left is an

3. outline. What remains
   in my hands are
   someone else's memories,

4. something severed.
   At some point, we will

5. kill everything, but the
   memories will be the
   only living thing.

· *Father (far left) in Taiwan* ·

Dear Father,

You don't know this, but yesterday we moved you to a new facility. You were kicked out of the other one for trying to escape too many times, for being too restless. When we arrived at the new facility, I unbuckled your seatbelt and watched you pull it all the way out, let it go, pull it out again. Then you tried to buckle the metal part into the door.

I watched you for a while, didn't help, because I am not a good daughter. Because you have become an example of how the brain loses everything but its gilded frame.

I left you with the new caretaker, whose name is Winnie, the same name as your ten-year-old granddaughter. But you wouldn't know that. I told Winnie, who was still in that state of unknowing, all about you. I knew that when I would see her again, her face would be torn.

We cleaned out your old room while you explored your new home. One child placed a few tiny teapots on the table, to take with her. You don't remember, but Mother used to collect tiny teapots. Wherever I went, I bought her a small teapot.

The teapots were my words. Each could be combined with others to form sentences. By the time she died, Mother had boxes of mini teapots from all over the world. The more I bought her, the more she refined what she wanted. *It's better if the lids come off,* she said. *It's better if the spout's hole is open.* By the time she died, she had finally figured out the perfect teapot. By the time we die, we know everything we need to know.

When she died, I threw most things away, except for the teapots. When a mother dies, everything you've given to her comes back to you. Now the teapots line up on my mantel like grief.

Father, I left all of your books on the shelf for the next resident. I didn't recognize most of the books, ones passed on by other dead people's families. This was the eighth time we moved you. The first time, we needed a large moving truck and four movers. The first time is when I herniated a few discs lifting a table. I know this pain isn't grief though, because I can feel it and identify its source.

The first time was ten years ago. The first time, we left your brain behind. Sometimes I wonder what your brain is doing now. If the new owners of your home recognized it as a brain or mistook it for one of the hundreds of donut peaches in the backyard and ate it.

This time, we moved two chairs, some photo albums, and some clothing. We moved the small kitchen table into our garage. Last time, we moved the bed into a child's room. The time before that, a couch into storage. Dying always seems to involve moving furniture.

When I returned to the new facility, Winnie was missing half of her face. She told us about your constipation, how you had become angry and shoved her, how eventually she just let you soil yourself as you kneeled next to your new bed. I imagined you kneeling, as if in prayer. Soiling yourself against God.

When I came by, you were sitting on the small twin bed, back facing us, staring out at the new view. We talked about you as if you weren't there. You, lost in the sky's blue straitjacket. Winnie said you were calm now. I corrected her, *calm* for *now*.

In the great room, a frail man with white hair lay on the couch chewing the blanket's corner. Another woman sat with her mouth open, body curled in a way that seemed permanent. This is how I imagined executed bodies underground, freshly tossed, frozen in various positions.

Another woman saw me and leaned in, *You wouldn't believe what they're doing to me here.*

I went up and down the hallways, reading bios about the football player, the CEO of a toy company, the teacher, the engineer, and all I could think about was all the history trapped in one building. Winnie led you into the dining area and I snuck out, like so many times before, knowing you wouldn't remember that I was ever there. I didn't look back. Feelings had become useless.

Later that night, we played basketball in our neighborhood park. We played horse, laughing at our airballs. We pointed to the big white building on the hill where you are now staying. I imagined you sitting on the twin bed, staring out the window at the city lights, not knowing you were staring out at us. And I wondered how many more times you would die.

Someone threw me a basketball. I was at H-O-R-S, losing a game I usually won easily. And I thought of what Sarah Manguso wrote in *The Two Kinds of Decay*: *You can learn only from moving forward at the rate you are moved, as brightness, into brightness.*[xviii] I turned back to the net and took a shot into the darkness, into the brightness.

OPTIONAL BATHS

OPTION A   OPTION B

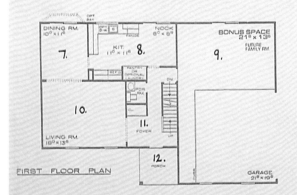

FIRST FLOOR PLAN

The Oxford

SECOND FLOOR

1. ME: WHEN DID YOU
   COME TO AMERICA?
2. MOTHER: 1964. I CAME FOR
   GRADUATE SCHOOL.
3. WHY DID YOU LEAVE TAIWAN?
4. I DON'T KNOW. ALL MY
   FRIENDS WERE LEAVING.
5. WHAT WERE YOU DOING IN
   TAIWAN AT THE TIME?
6. I WAS WORKING IN THE
   GOVERNMENT.

FIRST FLOOR

7. WHERE DID YOU ATTEND
   GRADUATE SCHOOL?
8. YOU DON'T NEED TO
   WRITE IT DOWN.
9. WHY NOT?
10. IT'S A SMALL SCHOOL
    CALLED APPALACHIAN STATE.
11. DID YOU PLAN TO STAY
    IN AMERICA?
12. OH NO NO NO.

- Unique bonus space home

- Bonus space expands into super-rumpus room.
  Buy it already finished, or finish it when you need it as a dormitory bedroom
  and bath, 4th bedroom and bath, family room.

- Full Basement • Central hall foyer entrance • 2-car garage

PRICE _____ Including Base Lot   Side Entrance Garage

FOX RUN GREEN — WEST BLOOMFIELD TOWNSHIP — 851-6550

Dear Teacher,

Once I asked you if poets need to suffer. I had made a habit of this question. You said that the notion was ridiculous and that there are so many great poets who lived tepid lives, such as Shakespeare, Stevens, Merwin, Moore, and Chaucer.

You also said that it can be dangerous to think that the tortured lives of Roethke, Plath, Keats, or Milton are somehow models for poets. I asked you that question because so many of the contemporary poets who seemed to write the haunted poetry that I was drawn to, had seemingly not just suffered, but truly *suffered*.

Once when I was at a writer's conference, a well-known poet came up to a few of us on a porch and joined our conversation. This startled me. His eyes fixed on one particular woman, making a cathedral of her, and all the surrounding buildings simply disappeared.

I recognized that look. I have looked longingly at photos of writers or celebrities and wondered about them. I've never forgotten the way he focused so much on the woman, on catching her eye. At the time, I just wanted attention, for the poet to look at me in the way he looked at her.

Once you wrote me to tell me that while you felt like I could write a capable and competent poem, you thought I was too impatient. You told me that writing takes patience and focus. And that it takes time. And that I should demand more of my poems.

You also told me that writing poems isn't a contest or a competitive sport, that there's no finish line to cross. I thought about this—I knew that there was no finish line, but if there were, I would be tempted to try and cross it first.

When I asked you how I could write poems like the ones this woman at the conference had written, you wrote more about suffering. That there's actual suffering and the empathy for the suffering of others. But none of those things matter as much as being able to work through, over, and under the conflicts within a poem. You told me how poetry emerges out of a poet's working out of the conflicts. And this working out needed to be artful, earned, and authentic.

You also told me that if I were acutely aware and awake to the world around me, there would be enough trauma and existential pain to last me a lifetime. I'm not sure I believed you at the time, but what you said gave me permission to keep writing, even if I didn't believe I had suffered enough, or in ways that others had, in the way that the woman at the conference had.

Decades have passed since we talked about this. Since then I have learned that we all suffer, in our own ways, some times more than other times. When my mother died, I wondered why so many people whose mothers had died could go on living. I have rain in my eyes and can no longer see. My eyelids are now umbrellas.

I've since realized that it was the art this woman made that resonated with the poet. Not her suffering. Once I could see that, I never envied anyone's suffering again. As time went on, I realized that I wanted to write poems so I could make someone feel something. I wanted something I had written, or how I had written it, to compel someone to want to find me, so badly that they were willing to disappear.

I began to admire work where language enacted subject matter, not where content overwhelmed or trumped language. The poet Richard Siken said something similar: *My contribution isn't going to be the biographical facts. It will be my take on it.*[xix] I think that's true for all of us, our *take on it.*

The paradox is that we don't actually *take* anything. Writing feels a bit like trying to attach words to things that are moving, that we cannot see, and that we can never fully understand.

Maybe I am staring into a piece of paper like it is a pond, hoping one day that what looks back is not my own reflection, but my great-grandmother's face. Maybe poetry is the distance between my face and her face. Maybe it's the difference between how the moon looks in the sky and how it contorts when a mayfly travels across the pond.

Guest Check

PERSONS	SERVER	TABLE	CHECK 01240

Me: When you came to America, where did you land?

Mother: I landed in LA. My classmate let me stay for a night. Then I got on a Greyhound bus to Dallas. I then got on another plane. Because I couldn't speak English, I didn't know I had to switch planes. The steward had to call me off because I just sat there.

GLOBE TICKET COMPANY 495

Guest Check

PERSONS	SERVER	TABLE	CHECK 01240

Mother: When I got to Atlanta, there were no planes so they put me in a hotel for the night. I was scared because I didn't know how to use anything.

Me: Like what?

Mother: Eating. Ordering. I watched a person next to me order toast and orange juice so I ordered the same thing.

GLOBE TICKET COMPANY 495

Me: What didn't you know how to use in the hotel?

Mother: The shower. Which was hot, which was cold. I also put a chair in front of the door. It opened right onto the road. I was very very scared.

GLOBE TICKET COMPANY 495

Dear Daughter,

Sometimes I wish I hadn't tried to fix everything from your childhood. Sometimes I wish I hadn't tried so hard to help you memorize your multiplication facts when you weren't ready.

Sometimes I wonder how many mistakes I am making now that will only become clearer later.

When I was in high school, my parents and their friends would compare what colleges their children had gotten into. *She's going to Stanford*, boasted my mother about my sister. *How about this one*, an auntie pointed to me. *This one . . .*, my mother said, and shook her head.

In my dreams, I always made my mother proud. When she died, all my dreams disappeared. They flew away like forty-four birds into the sky. When she died, I felt a sheet lift up over my head. When I looked up, the birds each had a section in their beaks that they carried away.

I have spent a lifetime believing that the main thing that mattered was being smart. I have spent your lifetime, just twelve years, finding an exit from this corridor.

Yesterday, I heard a noise in the sky and saw birds fighting—two crows against one. And I wondered, does the smarter crow always win? Did you know that crows can count to three and parrots can count up to six? Would a parrot win against a crow?[XX]

Did you know that Chinese fishermen allowed cormorants to eat every eighth fish the birds caught? Once the cormorants caught seven, they ignored an order to dive and refused to move, as if they were waiting for their reward, the eighth fish. As if they were counting.[xxi]

Daughter, each day I am tired of thinking about intelligence. Each day I am tired of worrying about intelligence. I despise my obsession with intelligence. *You have to do better than Americans,* my mother always said. *Ta men hui qiao bu qi ni,* she said, *or they will look down on you.* Striving for intelligence can feel like a fight to be seen. In this way, striving is a political act. But the costs of striving are high. The system and its goals are established by others, so there's never an end to striving.

Plus, the stereotype that Asian Americans are good at math and/or are intelligent can be harmful not only to Asian Americans (who don't meet or choose not to meet certain rigid expectations) but also to other BIPOC (by pitting marginalized people against each other).

In *Minor Feelings,* Cathy Park Hong writes about the book and film *Crazy Rich Asians: If you discriminate against us, we'll make more money than you and buy your fancy hotel that wouldn't let us in. Capitalism as retribution for racism. But isn't that how whiteness recruits us? Whether it's through retribution or indebtedness, who are we when we become better than them in a system that destroyed us?*[xxii]

I often think about what Susan Sontag once said: *I don't care about someone being intelligent; any situation between people, when they are really human with each other, produces "intelligence."*[xxiii] Dwelling on whether to care or not to care is a privilege. I agree with Sontag in principle, but agreeing with something isn't the same as believing it or experiencing it.

I agree that I am American, but don't believe it. I agree that I am Chinese, but don't believe it. I agree that I'm a writer, but whether I believe it or not often doesn't depend on me. I agree that the man in the wheelchair is my father, but I no longer believe it. I agree that my mother is dead, but I don't believe it.

Recently at breakfast at an arts colony, some American artists who live abroad said, *You don't feel American until you leave America.* I thought of all my trips to Taiwan and China to try to be amongst my people and how everyone just emphatically called me *American.* Does this mean I won't feel alive until I'm dead?

Dear Daughter, yesterday the facility called about your grandfather again. They gave him a stack of papers and made him a badge that said he was the head of the walking club. There's a shadow of intelligence in him still. The shadow is in pursuit of the body, but the body has gone overseas.

I chase the shadow with my scissors, try to cut the shadow from the body once and for all. So that we can finally be free from intelligence, finally be free. But when the shadow blows back into the sea, it pulls me with it.

ME: WHAT DID YOU DO IN NYC? MOTHER: I WAS WORKING AT A CHINESE SHIPPING COMPANY BUT IT WAS SO FAR AND I HAD TO RIDE THE SUBWAY AND MY ENGLISH WAS NOT VERY GOOD. ME: DID FATHER GO TO MONTICELLO TOO? MOTHER: YES. MANY OF US CHINESE WENT. ME: WHAT DID YOU DO? MOTHER: I WAS A CHAMBER MAID, I CLEANED TOILETS, ROOMS. ME: WERE PEOPLE NICE? MOTHER: YES, BECAUSE WE WERE FOREIGNERS. WE WERE STRANGE.

ME: WHAT DID YOU DO AFTER GRAD SCHOOL? MOTHER: I WENT TO NEW YORK CITY TO DA GONG [WORK]. IT WAS THE WORLD'S FAIR IN 1964. ME: WHERE DID YOU WORK? MOTHER: PEOPLE WENT TO THE MOUNTAINS IN NEW YORK IN THE SUMMER SO I WENT TO FIND WORK TOO. ME: DO YOU REMEMBER THE NAME? MOTHER: SUMMIT HOTEL? MONTICELLO, NEW YORK.

ME: IS THAT WHERE YOU MET FATHER? MOTHER: YES. THERE WERE A LOT OF NICE CHINESE BOYS IN NEW YORK CITY AT THAT TIME. ME: WHERE DID YOU LIVE? MOTHER: WE SQUEEZED INTO AN APARTMENT. I STILL REMEMBER: 112 BROADWAY.

Broadway – North – West 111th Streets

Dear Ford Motor Company,

Father started working with you on November 10, 1966, four years before I was born. Growing up, I saw your navy oval symbol everywhere. On keychains, sweatshirts, notepads, pencils, on all of our cars. In my driveway now, there are two Ford cars.

After my mother died, I found a box with your papers in it. In that box were two letters from you. One dated January 10, 1992. Someone had hand-written in the "1" in 1992. Someone didn't want to waste paper or time to reprint the letter.

When I lifted the paper up toward the light, I could see a Ford watermark in the middle. If you lift me up toward the light, you can see a Ford watermark in my chest.

The letter says:

> Dear Fu
>
> Ken Dabrowski and I would like to congratulate you on your perfect attendance record for 1991. This significant achievement takes personal dedication and an attitude of loyalty, teamwork and cooperativeness for which I express my genuine gratitude.
>
> Sincerely,
> R. H. Schaffart

The second letter, dated February 8, 1994, states:

> Dear Fu:
>
> Congratulations! You made it in 1993-Perfect Attendance. I appreciate your dedication.
>
> Loyalty, teamwork and cooperation contribute to the Ford Motor goal of improvement in everything we do, and you have proved this by your 1993 Perfect Attendance.
>
> A. Iaconelli

I wonder how many of these letters R. H. Schaffart and A. Iaconelli signed. I wonder how many people achieved perfect attendance each year. I graduated from the University of Michigan in 1992 and entered graduate school after that. My sister graduated from Stanford University in 1991 and entered law school after that. While we were busy overeducating ourselves, Father was showing up to work every single day.

I imagine him sitting at a metal desk in a cubicle, trying to figure out how to exhibit American *loyalty, teamwork, and cooperativeness.*

I remember going to Father's office once. I think this was when he had gotten promoted. I remember his talking about Ford and the people he worked with. I remember the ambition and wildness in his voice. Sometimes tinged with anger, sometimes with frustration. Now that I'm older, I can imagine his not understanding the English clichés, idioms—all the cultural differences.

Dear Ford Motor Company, do you know that I didn't learn the phrase *the straw that broke the camel's back* until college? I've never heard Father say *miss the boat* or *time to hit the sack* or *it's not rocket science* or *pull yourself together* or *time flies when you're having fun* or *wrap your head around something* or *a bird in the hand is worth two in the bush* . . .

Somewhere along the way, I picked up some idioms from other people. From *Scooby Doo*. From *Inspector Gadget*. *The Brady Bunch*. *Gilligan's Island*. And from my favorite, *The Love Boat*, where everyone was always falling in love until the boat docked. Because landing meant giving up the past.

Dear Ford Motor Company, I've always thanked you for giving Father a desk. A lamp. An office. A computer. I've always thanked you for giving me my desk. My lamp. My office. My computer. For allowing me to speak out of silence, when silenced, and when I have silenced myself.

I still have a Ford Motor Company stapler on my desk. I've always thanked you for stapling my family to this country. But sometimes I can't help feeling as if I'm a woodcut of this country. And that you are the woodcutter.

Now that I'm older, I have thought harder about assimilation, realized that assimilation has a price. I have thought more about who gets to assimilate and why, about the downsides of assimilation, what's lost during the gains. And that assimilation is often largely economic, not political or cultural.

Only today do I have the language to understand that assimilation means adopting dominant norms and ideals such as whiteness. And that since assimilation is ultimately unachievable, there is always a gap, a space of estrangement.

I've also since thought harder about all those consecutive days Father worked, his perfect attendance and the idea that we strive to fill or complete things as a form of assimilation, that assimilation, like overeducating myself, is an endless pursuit. I've since come to think that maybe emptying out is the beautiful thing. The space between the raindrops. The space where I live. The space where Father now lives and where he will die.

Body Engineering
Ford Motor Company

P.O. Box 2053
Dearborn, Michigan 48121

February 8, 1994

Mr. F. Chang

Dear Fu:

Congratulations! You made it in 1993-Perfect Attendance. I appreciate your dedication.

Loyalty, teamwork and cooperation contribute to the Ford Motor goal of improvement in everthing we do, and you have proved this by your 1993 Perfect Attendance.

A. Iaconelli

Was this your first job?
Look at the window
behind you, as if leaving
a country was all
perspective and light.
I wonder what is in your hand.
It's so thin and small,
it must be my home.

Body Engineering
Ford Motor Company

P.O. Box 2053
Dearborn, Michigan 48121

January 10, 1992

Mr. F. Chang

Dear Fu

Ken Dabrowski and I would like to congratulate you on your perfect attendance record for 1991. This significant achievement takes personal dedication and an attitude of loyalty, teamwork and cooperativeness for which I express my genuine gratitude.

Sincerely,

R. H. Schaffart

Dear Daughter,

What I didn't tell you is that I sat in the front row of the reading, ready to smile and to give a good introduction like a good host. What I didn't tell you is that when the reader had a white character call an Asian American one a *squinty-eyed feckless cunt*, I remembered all the times when others took their fingers and pulled their eyes wide into a horizon. All the times people yelled *Chink!* to my family or me. The time someone wrote *Chink* on our driveway in chalk.

What I didn't tell you is that the reader intimidated me with his confidence. That my mother never taught me how to speak to white people, to loud white people. Shake the hands of confident white people. Speak in front of white people. At a lectern. With a white piece of paper with black type on it.

What I didn't tell you is that I envied Joan Didion, not only for her writing but also because she had things passed down to her, that she knew what her great-great-great-great-great-grandparents did. I identified more with Nora Krug, when she wrote: *In my mind, a family began with one's parents and ended with oneself.*[xxiv]

What I didn't tell you is that after the reader's comment, I wondered if I should have gotten up and gone to the bathroom. Whether I should have cried in the bathroom. I wondered how to fight my urge to take the microphone away from him.

Instead, I stared at my dark Taiwanese hands from Father, my long thin Northern Chinese hands from Mother. I was furious at my hands. At myself. At my history. At my inability to do anything with those hands. I was upset that my mother and father didn't spray the chalk off our driveway, instead waiting for the sun to erase it. Not erased, the word etched into my skin.

What I didn't tell you is that I got up to introduce another poet I had been looking forward to meeting. And then I sat down. My hands illuminated atop the lectern, white for just a few seconds, then brown again.

Dear Daughter, I did tell you what happened, and it was only after I had told you, after you had gone to bed, that I wonder if I had wrongly passed my pain onto you. Wrongly wept my tears into your body. I wondered if you suffer like I do, in school, on the playground, in class, with your teachers, looking at ads, watching TV. Or do you not suffer like I do?

You were born in a more diverse and progressive state. You are half Asian and half white. Does that mean you experience half the racism? That you feel half the pain? Or, alongside your own pain, do you inherit all of your grandmother's pain, my pain, America's pain?

I thought hard about whether to stay silent. About whether to tell you. Staying silent was following in my mother's footsteps. But by telling you, I risked adversely shaping your views of the world—as an unfair one, as a racist one, as one where we would be victims.

I've since thought harder about why I was so upset. The racial slur had been dropped into a piece with no apparent purpose and thus never transcended its own racism. In that way, the randomness of the slur was affirming the slur itself, as well as negative stereotypes of Asian American women. I could tell you more about the aftermath and the response of the writer and his friend but then I'd have to relive those dreadful experiences.

Do you remember the boy on the patio? How he pulled his eyes wide at us and suddenly the same thin line? Do you remember what I said to the boy? *You don't want to make fun of people for what they look like, right?* The boy, maybe ten, our friend's child, someone you had played with many times before, just laughed. Do you know how hard it was for me to speak up, even to a ten-year-old? Do you know how astonished I was that so much had changed but so much hadn't?

If I don't know how to protect myself, how can I protect you? I know that even though I was born on this land, in a small hospital in Detroit, Michigan, that my sun is still brittle. That if my sun even exists, it is behind all the other suns and emits radio static.

I promise not to pass handfuls of hate into your hands. I promise to teach you how to be the bird and the beak. And the sky with many other birds.

The next morning, we ate breakfast, got you ready for camp, ignored the loud hawk that circled above the cabin. When I grabbed my computer bag and opened the front door, a bright white triangular light blinded us. And we moved through it.

IT IS A VIOLATION OF THE U. S. CODE (AND PUNISHABLE AS SUCH) TO COPY, PRINT, PHOTOGRAPH, OR OTHERWISE ILLEGALLY USE THIS CERTIFICATE.

THE UNITED STATES OF AMERICA

No. 8999897

CERTIFICATE OF NATURALIZATION

Petition No. 302840

·ORIGINAL·

Personal description of holder as of date of naturalization· Date of birth April 6, 1941 sex Female;
complexion Medium color of eyes Dark Brown color of hair Black height 5 feet 3 inches;
weight 130 pounds visible distinctive marks None
Marital status Married Country of former nationality China
I certify that the description above given is true, and that the photograph affixed hereto is a likeness of me.

Jeng Chang
(Complete and true signature of holder)

EASTERN DISTRICT OF MICHIGAN } ss:
SOUTHERN DIVISION

Be it known, that at a term of the District Court of
The United States
held pursuant to law at Detroit
on February 26, 1973 the Court having found that
Jeng Chang
then residing at 14595 Yorkshire Street, Southgate, Michigan 48195
intends to reside permanently in the United States (when so required by the
Naturalization Laws of the United States) had in all other respects complied with
the applicable provisions of such naturalization laws, and was entitled to be
admitted to citizenship, thereupon ordered that such person be and she was
admitted as a citizen of the United States of America.
In testimony whereof the seal of the court is hereunto affixed this 26th.
day of February in the year of our Lord, nineteen hundred and
Seventy-three.

jco

Clerk of the U.S District Court.
By Deputy Clerk.

Seal

IT IS A VIOLATION OF THE U. S. CODE (AND PUNISHABLE AS SUCH) TO
COPY, PRINT, PHOTOGRAPH, OR OTHERWISE ILLEGALLY USE THIS CERTIFICATE.

DEPARTMENT OF JUSTICE

中華民國內政部國民身分證用專用章

Dear Father,

In her letter to Dr. and Mrs. J. G. Holland, Emily Dickinson wrote, *I write to you. I receive no letter.* Dear Father, why does Mother keep dusting the stars? I write to her too. But I receive no letter. You don't read my letters either. Sometimes I think it would be easier if grief were no longer blurred. If I could just ride it like a horse.

Father, other times I'm so happy to have the frame that holds your organs even if when you look at me, all you see is flickering. When I look at you, I imagine myself inside your head, looking out at me, something that is not you, but of you. Someone you recently called your wife or your mother. And now call nothing.

I know you haven't read *H Is for Hawk* by Helen Macdonald, because you can't read, but she writes about the death of her father so well: *The archaeology of grief is not ordered. It is more like earth under a spade, turning up things you had forgotten. Surprising things come to light: not simply memories, but states of mind, emotions, older ways of seeing the world.*[XXV]

When someone has dementia, or any brain disease, grief is multidimensional. You grieve them while you are wiping their nose or cutting their food into small limbs. Part of them is dead, part of them is dying. But so much of them is still alive. It's like Macdonald's earth, but that person is only partially buried. Every time you turn the spade, you poke them and they try and get up, wander around until you have to rebury them, tuck them back into the earth. I have had so many funerals for you, Father. I hide my hands in my pockets because they are always covered with dirt.

Yesterday, you wandered into another resident's room and got into a fight. You lost the fight. Do you remember how tall you are? 5'5" and 140 pounds. Do you know how tall the men in your facility are? Much taller than you.

By the time I was able to get to the ER, your face was all swollen on one side, lip bloody and ballooned, shirt ripped. No one witnessed the fight, but I heard that you had wandered into the wrong room. I've never seen you fight anyone, never a bruise on your body.

I've only seen you get angry in public once—my junior year in college when you were trying to negotiate a lower price for a rug for my apartment. The salesperson told you to *go back to China*, and you yelled back. I wonder how many times you've wanted to show anger like that but couldn't, wouldn't. I wonder how many times you have been told to go back to a country that wasn't even yours.

I remember Mother hunched over your hospital bed, after your stroke, the last time you had your own brain. The last time we had our own brains. Before Mother died, she said, *Who will take care of him?* There was a father. Then there wasn't a father.

Mother knew everything. Mother hoarded everything, even history. Those who know everything always seem to die first. There was a mother. Then there wasn't a mother. There was a history. Then there wasn't a history.

Dear Father, if I were really Chinese, I would have you live at home with me. Mother knew that I wasn't a real Chinese person.

Secretly I was happy to hear that the other man also had a bruise on his face. This means you at least got one punch in. This means you fought back. This means I am not a good person. They won't tell me who the man is, but today

I will find the man with the bruise on his face. I will smile at the bruise. The bruise will not smile back.

I learned later that shortly after your fight, the man died. You were his final fight. Maybe he confused you with death.

I'm sorry for doing a terrible job caring for you. I think Mother knew I wouldn't do a good job. I want to tell her that I want so badly to be a part of this world, to stand in it, but every hand I touch withholds warmth. The world gathers everywhere beyond me. Is this how Mother felt too? Invisible to everyone but you, but also invisible to you.

Mother would be glad to know that yesterday Diane was able to go to the ER with you. Diane was diagnosed with cancer when she was eighteen and was given three weeks to live. Diane is fifty-five. She was told she would never have children. She has a thirty-three-year-old son. I now know more about Diane's history than Mother's history, than your history. Diane held my hand in the ER like a mother would. Like Mother never did.

You can tell when someone has suffered deeply. Their heart is smaller and it no longer smokes. I want my heart to be smaller, too, more used up. When I look down at my heart, it is no longer there. I find it kneeling in the corner and shaking. I tell it in Chinese to stand up, but it doesn't understand me. When I command it in English, it only gets larger.

Like Mother, I always have snacks in my purse. At the ER, I handed you a Kit Kat. Your mouth made noises that only a mouth God made could make. You knew what you were eating. You knew you had eaten it before. You knew you liked it. I dug through my purse as if I were looking for Mother's body. I gave you another and another until my purse was empty.

1. ME: DO YOU REGRET COMING TO AMERICA? HOW ABOUT FATHER?

2. MOTHER: YES. IT'S NOT THAT GREAT HERE. IT'S BEEN HARD FOR US. BUT WHEN WE GO BACK, NOTHING FEELS FAMILIAR EITHER.

3. FATHER WOULD HAVE DONE BETTER IN TAIWAN. IT'S HARDER FOR HIM HERE BECAUSE HE IS STILL CHINESE. HE ISN'T AMERICAN.

Dear B,

You walked by in a white button-down and slacks and I hopped up, happy to see you at a reading. A woman passed by to tell me how much she liked the poems I had just read. She told you she enjoyed your reading too. You looked down, began texting someone, your face like a ticker tape, the words on your phone glowing across it.

But he didn't read, I said, confused.

Oh, I'm so sorry. It's been a long few days and I'm tired, she said. And then she did what many of us do when we make mistakes. She kept on talking. *Where do you live? I'm certain I've seen you read somewhere else then. When did you move away? What year was it? I'm certain I've seen you read.*

I was there. I am certain you did not read. I am certain it was K who read. I am certain that K is nearly two times taller than you. I am certain K is wider than you. I am certain K was wearing glasses.

I am uncertain if K was wearing a jacket. Uncertain if K was wearing dress shoes or sneakers. Uncertain how K felt while he was reading. Uncertain if K was wearing something around his neck.

When the woman finally left, you were angry. You were so angry I told you my story, a story I hadn't planned to tell anyone. Three nights before, I read with other poets. I was part of the first group to read. Another Asian American poet also read in the first group. A different person introduced each group.

After the reading, the second introducer came up to me and said: *All your books sold out. I'll get it at the book fair. I enjoyed your poems so much.*

I didn't bring any books, I said. *My book isn't out yet.* She said: *I'm sorry. Oh right, you read those OBIT poems. Oh I love those. They are so moving.* And then she kept on talking.

The conference hadn't even started yet. I went back to my hotel room and wanted to pound my fists on something, but when I looked down, my hands had turned into flowers. I spent the rest of the night alone, watching them die.

Why bother writing when people can't even tell us apart, I asked you. This wasn't the first time that I had been mistaken for another Asian poet, writer, or person. When we were outside, waiting for our rides, you told K the story. In that moment, the three of us were connected in a way that we didn't want to be.

As I got into my car and the driver said my name, I heard you talking to K about this still. I was certain I heard you talking to K about this. I'm uncertain how much longer you talked about this. I'm uncertain if K replied. I am certain this harmed you. Because I am much older than you, I am certain you will be harmed many more times in your life. I am certain you will silence yourself many more times. I am certain the driver and I moved on. We talked about the meth and heroin epidemic in the city. But I didn't forget this woman. Her mouth filled with our words.

This week, so many friends saw me. They looked at me and knew who I was. They called my name. They touched my hands which were no longer hands. Why did I mostly remember the two white women then? Because this country is a harness for us, B. We can put it on. But other people have to take it off.

Do you know that I, too, make these mistakes? That I once called a Black woman the name of the woman sitting next to her. I was certain I was nervous. Certain I was new to the job. Certain there were twenty-five new people in the room. Certain that I had snuffed them out, erased them, exiled them. That I had harmed them, that I needed to do better.

Do you know that at the same conference, a poet of color confused an Asian American poet with another Asian American poet? When it was pointed out to her, she laughed it off. B, each confusion is a decapitation.

Why do we bother then? Do you remember what you said to me right before the woman walked by? You were telling me about form. How the form of my poems inspired your poems. We were talking about our poems. You were telling me how you were planting diamonds on the page. And then the miner came by and blew the diamonds out of our eyes. And we were again left with two black holes.

I was happy to hear that something I made helped you make something new. That moment isn't gone. I brought it home with me. I put it on a hanger in my closet.

I don't know if you know that Charles Simic once said: *The world is beautiful but not sayable. That's why we need art.*[xxvi] I think that's why we need *all* art. Not just art from some people. Or whether you know what Osip Mandelstam said: *What tense would you choose to live in? I want to live in the imperative of the future passive participle—in the 'what ought to be.'*[xxvii] That's where I want to live too—in the *what ought to be*. I don't know where this is or what it looks like, but I know somehow it begins with language.

國家圖書館出版品預行編目資料入館圖書閱覽專用中華民國總統內政部

Dear Father,

Yesterday I needed to find your Medicare number and I couldn't find it. Yesterday I searched through files and boxes. Yesterday I learned that you had an American name, *Peter*.

On the social security card, it says you lived at 4109 Walnut St., Phila., Pa. 19104. Your signature looked like you were learning how to write cursive. I imagined you with your round head, bent down, signing in one continuous, strained motion, without lifting the pen.

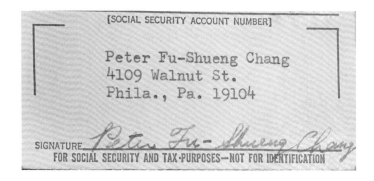

In the same box, I found my first social security card. I, too, was learning how to write cursive. I marveled at how you and I both wrote in perfect cursive when asked for a signature. I, too, wasn't sure what to call myself so I wrote it twice. My *M* is for *Ming-Kai*, my Chinese name. Look how it's hidden. Look how *Peter* gets to sit in the front.

I wonder why I never heard you say your name was Peter, never heard anyone call you *Peter*. I heard that the nice elderly people who housed Mother when she first came to this country called her *Felicity* because she smiled so much.

I hardly ever remember Mother smiling or laughing. My memories of Mother were of her frowning. Now I know. She left things in other countries. Like a bird who sheds a wet feather without knowing it. And the joy of the child who finds the feather. The joy stays with the child. The bird keeps moving.

On another card, someone crossed out *Peter*. I wonder when this was. I wonder why you gave up your future.

Yesterday I finished the book *Five Days Gone: The Mystery of My Mother's Disappearance as a Child* by Laura Cumming. Cumming investigates her family history and learns about her mother's story and background, how her mother was kidnapped by her grandmother for five days. Her mother's story is a skein of secrets and discovery.

After I shut the book I grieved all the details of our lives that disappear like geese. That maybe we only see any bird once. That seeing a new bird is an elegy.

I marveled at how Cumming could speak the same language as the people who might know her family's secrets, how she could read documents in English, how she could trace the geese through language.

There's so much I would like to know about geese—what it feels like to go in and out of weather, in and out of history, of time. Father, I am ashamed by how much I yearn. Father, I grieve in acres. This land is a facade for the land I really come from. There are lands behind lands.

When I grieve for Mother, I think I am also grieving for my history. I want to fly perfectly above my history like geese. I want to watch the cities pass as I go from one to another. But all the people have no faces. My eyes are deciduous.

Dear Father, or Peter, do you know that 4109 Walnut St., Phila., Pa. 19104 is now a Homewood Suites? I imagine how many people have slept in your dreams since then.

I follow the Google car's path with its big camera on the roof. I see a woman pulling a wagon with a child in it. I see the woman wave to someone, her hand frozen in midair.

Someday, when the woman is dead, the woman's daughter may find the photo and wonder what her mother was doing that day on that street. She may not remember her mother or the street. But she may remember the wagon and the creaky sound it made when it moved.

Father, I wonder what you were doing there. Was that where you landed when you first came to America? Was this your first address? I will never know. But I now know what your cursive looked like, what the street looked like, that you once had an American name. That you once had American dreams.

Dear Y,

Do you remember once in San Francisco it began to rain? And then you began to dance? And that childish boyish grin and dimple, your arms up in the air, walking backward, swaying sideways, always smiling. I wondered how a poet could be so joyful.

Another time, in San Clemente, we had ordered big salads. I don't remember our talk, but I remember the weight of my parents' illnesses. I wanted so badly for something to change, but I was anaesthetized on time's operating table.

Once we met at a fancier restaurant and sat in a booth to the side. My eyes hurt then too. I couldn't yet see beyond Mother's illness or my grief. Father's dementia. But there we were, sitting slightly elevated in an uncomfortable booth, beyond everything, even sadness.

We only talked about poetry. For hours and hours. *What are you reading,* you always asked. I would answer and you would look at me with your mouth open, head to the side, while the people around us came and went.

There was something beautiful about our exchanges, our wobbling necks, leaning out and back in, always back in. We spoke against gravity. Poets and poems came out of mouths faster than we could comprehend each other. We could hear the clocks, but their ticking had separated from death.

Tiny bulbs of wisdom came out of your mouth. *What's the rush,* you said about publishing. I added: *Does the world need another competent book of poems?* Most times, we wouldn't answer our own questions because what did we know? We only knew that we couldn't scrub poetry off our bodies. And we ourselves feared the greatest death, which was writing merely competent poems.

What I've learned from you is how important friends are to the poems themselves. Do you remember how we would bring each other's manuscripts, lean
down and read our own scribbles, try to explain to each other what we felt
was working and what wasn't? I admired how quickly you took poems in.
Who you were reading, what you had read, your philosophy on poetics, all
influenced my own thinking and my poems.

Once, after a literary reception, we sat on a bench indoors. *What are you
working on?* you asked. *I'm still working on the same manuscript. It's in my
purse.* I carried it around with me everywhere just in case I would have a
few minutes to work on it. You asked, *Can I see it?* You wore a gray suit
with a red tie that popped out. These were not poem-reading clothes. But
you insisted.

So I pulled out the manuscript. You opened it and started reading, your finger-
tips crossing the words, touching them as you might touch a body. *This one.
This is good.* You'd double tap and look up at me. No more smiling.

Head down, your fingers would travel to the next one. *This is very beautiful.*
You'd double tap the ending. Again and again, you read and told me what
you thought, what else I might read. I jotted down notes as quickly as I could.

People in work clothes came and went, their shoes stabbing the glossy floor.
Occasionally, while you were reading, I would look up and catch the eye of
a person in a suit. They would be talking while walking and then stop and
stare, knowing that somehow we weren't meant to be seen.

At some point, the event ended and the planners came out from the room
with their boxes and name tags still on. *You're still here!* they laughed and

pointed at us. *Reading poems,* I said, not too loudly for fear they might take something away from us. We barely looked up, lost in some shaft of half-light. When I did look up again, a hundred years had passed and they were gone.

More recently, you asked me to drive up to the city because you were with your mother who was sick. We met at the mall. I know this was the fall of 2017 because I had just gotten a new job. *I hope they don't kill you. I hope you still have time to write,* you said. I now understand what you meant. A job like this is like a burning house you have to sleep in. Over and over. In fact, for a writer, any busy day job can feel like a burning house. All of my poems smell like smoke.

You gave me feedback on my manuscript. *I wish I had something to show you too,* you said. I knew your mother was very ill but you didn't want to speak of it. My own mother had been ill and had died a few years prior. I did not want to speak of it. We only talked about poems.

Because we knew the poem was the shooter, shotgun, bullet, and the body. It was life and death. There was no need for anything else.

Do you remember how we chuckled at what Terrance Hayes once said? *I wrote it so I wouldn't have to talk about it.* Eight months after my mother died, I wrote seventy-five poems in two weeks. But I rarely talked about her dying or death.

Dear Y, thank you for being such a good poetry friend. By finding friends like you, I had inadvertently located the general coordinates of myself.

You may not know that you recently startled me when you said: *I only have twenty years left at the most*. When I read alumni magazines, I go straight to the class notes and look at when people begin dying. Then I count the pages between that year and my year of graduation. There aren't too many pages left. And I weep into my hands, quietly. For you, for me, for all the dead poets, for your mother, my mother, my father, your father. And when I'm done crying, I pick up the pencil again, try and describe the way the sky knows how to turn from blue to black and then blue again.

Dear Reader,

Yesterday during dinner at a writer's colony, a fiction writer said, *I've never written about playing hockey, even though I did it for many years and reached a really high level.* Then a playwright across from me said, *Maybe you just aren't ready. Sometimes it's just not time yet.*

At breakfast this morning, I spoke to a poet about trauma and how neither of our mothers, both of whom had left their countries, rarely spoke about their pasts. My mother fled from China to Taiwan when she was eight or nine, and then left Taiwan for America when she was twenty-one or twenty-two. This poet said that *maybe it's us*, the next generation, who will write in response to that history.

I think the poet was right. To borrow Julia Creet's phrase, maybe *memory is where we have arrived rather than where we have left.*[xxviii] And *arrived* means here, in this country, and also in the imaginations of the next generation. I think the playwright was right too. Willing and summoning is like dragging a small unwilling dog toward a larger dog. When I drag, the dog looks italicized, muscles tight, tail down.

Dragging a not-yet-ready memory, thought, or feeling toward language too early feels something like the dog. I can move it, but it will be difficult. More and more, I think writing is not a choice but an act of patience. An act of listening to silence, into silence.

I'm thinking about what Rainer Maria Rilke said: *And it is not even enough to have memories. When there are many of them you must forget and have the great patience to wait for their return. For the memories themselves aren't yet it.*[xxix]

I used to think I was a transcriber of my own experiences and memories, adding an image here and there, but now I think I am more of a shaper. I take small fragments of imagery, memory, silence, and thought, and shape them with imaginary hands into something different. What's left doesn't need to have a firm, precise shape that resembles reality though. It can be unshapely. Splayed.

The epistolary form was a way for me to speak to the dead, the not-yet-dead, the sky, the wild turkey scurrying away, its white feathers waddling deeper into the woods, into myself, into a younger self, away from myself. Toward my dead mother. Toward my history. Toward Father's silence. Toward silence. Toward death.

One of the challenges of the epistolary form is that the people you are writing to can't write back. If these people, like my mother or father, are no longer alive or can't speak, that poses fewer ethical issues. But when people are still alive, there are more immediate ethical challenges, so I chose to maintain the anonymity of most of the people in this book. I also change important details about individuals. At some point, the actual details and the specific people no longer seemed so important.

While writing these letters, I found boxes of old photos in a storage facility. I placed a few in the book and wrote short poems in response to the photos. I also found a series of interviews that I had conducted with my mother in 2007. I can't explain why I had asked her to speak, but perhaps the interview offered a form in which to speak into and out of silence. I had no plans for the interview. Still, I told her I was working on an essay (which I wasn't). When I asked my mother to ask my father if he would speak to me, he refused and asked why I would do something so *useless*. Shortly after, he had a stroke and could no longer communicate.

I had forgotten about these interviews until after my mother died. And then it took me years to find the files on a computer. I found them only after most of this book was written. I am grateful my mother agreed, even if she was reluctant. I sprinkled bits of our interview throughout this book.

This was the only time my mother had ever spoken to me substantively about her past. There weren't a lot of extra words. I could see how memory works (and fails) in fragments as my mother answered my questions—describing images of pickled vegetables, a servant escaping, a mother holding the hand of the wrong child.

Working on these letters and listening to the interviews made me think that grief and memory are related. That memory, trying to remember, is also an act of grieving. In my mother's case, sometimes forgetting or silence was a way to grieve lost lands and to survive. In my case, trying to know someone else's memories, even if it's through imagination and within silence, is also a form of grieving.

As I began to write, though, my own memories started to return, and I began to trace in language some of my own painful childhood experiences, which I had always kept hidden. I realized I had to tell my stories in order to reflect on theirs because, while I had always thought our stories were separate, they were actually intimately connected. I realized my parents' histories not only shaped them, but also shaped me in ways that I only began to consider after they could no longer speak to me.

I began to think about how maybe my memories are never really just my memories but are fragments of memories and stories from others. And that memory, for many of us, is shaped by motion, movement, and migration.

After I finished writing this book, I began reading *Memory and Migration*, an anthology edited by Julia Creet and Andreas Kitzmann, where I learned about Marianne Hirsch's concept of *postmemory: Postmemory is a powerful form of memory precisely because its connection to its object or source is mediated not through recollection but through an imaginative investment and creation. Postmemory characterizes the experience of those who grow up dominated by narratives that preceded their birth, whose own belated stories are evacuated by the stories of the previous generation, shaped by traumatic events that can be neither fully understood nor re-created.*[xxx]

The concept of postmemory seems to encapsulate both this book and my own life experiences. In the same anthology, the visual artist Yvonne Singer, whose parents had left Hungary for Canada during World War II, so aptly wrote: *I was between worlds, alienated from the Canadian world of my peers and excluded from the history and culture of my parents, who placed a veil of secrecy on the past.*[xxxi]

Mother had no words. All we had was silence. How does one interact with silence? How does one not die of silence? Maybe my thinking has been wrong all along. Maybe silence is not something to interact with, to be filled in, but rather to let wash over you, to exist within. Maybe silence is its own form of language. Maybe silence is also a life lived. Maybe the unspoken can lead to the widest imagination. Maybe it's the most open text. The loudest form of speaking we have.

Maybe if I listen closely enough, the stone is a thought, the bell makes a sound without ringing, and I can hear children grow. Maybe our histories can never be fully known. Maybe curiosity is its own language.

After I finished writing this book, I also began to think about how, for an immigrant's child like myself, perhaps because identity can be based on an unreliable postmemory, identity relies on the making of a present—through every teacher, friend, even enemy, and through all the books I've read. Maybe the act of writing for someone like me, isn't about speaking, but about making a person.

In the end, these epistles brought me much sadness and shame to write, but the process was also joyful. I've always loved what Jeanette Winterson in *Art Objects* says about the chisel:

> The chisel must be capable of shaping any material however unlikely. It has to leave runnels of great strength and infinite delicacy. In her own hands, the chisel will come to feel light and assured, as she refines it to take her grip and no other. If someone borrows it, it will handle like a clumsy tool or perform like a trick. And yet to her, as she works with it and works upon it, it will become the most precise instrument she knows. There are plenty of tools a writer can beg or borrow, but her chisel she must make for herself, just as Michelangelo did. [xxxii]

I'm still learning how to make my own chisel, but everything I write, no matter how crude, is an experiment with my unfinished chisel. Each time I sit down, I pull out my imaginary chisel, listen to the words that come up, like eavesdropping, crane my neck into language, into memory, into silence. And each time I write, the chisel becomes more and more finished and distinctly mine. And with each word, I become more and more myself.

I've always thought

the coordinates of your

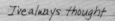

words are death.

When I finally find the

location, I learn that

there were never any

words there, just

blank paper, everywhere.

Notes

i   Bang, Mary Jo, *Elegy*, Graywolf Press, 2009, p. 63.

ii Ruefle, Mary, *Madness, Rack, and Honey: Collected Lectures*, Wave Books, 2012, p. 134.

iii Popova, Maria, "Donald Barthelme on the Art of Not-Knowing and the Essential Not-Knowing of Art", https://www.brainpickings. org/2014/04/07/donald-barthelme-not-knowing/.

iv Winterson, Jeanette, *Art Objects: Essays on Ecstasy and Effrontery*, Vintage, 1997, p. 169.

v   Pavlović, Srđja. "Memory for Breakfast." In *Memory and Migration: Multidisciplinary Approaches to Memory Studies*, edited by Julia Creet and Andreas Kitzmann, University of Toronto Press, 2014, p. 43.

vi Bishop, Elizabeth, *The Complete Poems: 1927-1979*, Farrar, Straus and Giroux, 1983.

vii Kuusisto, Stephen, *The Poet's Notebook*, W.W. Norton & Company, 1997, p. 228.

viii Bishop, *The Complete Poems: 1927-1979*, Farrar, Straus and Giroux, 1983.

ix Pavlović, p. 22.

x   Rushdie, Salman, *Shame*, Random House, 2008, p. 60.

xi Lee, Li-Young, *Breaking the Alabaster Jar: Conversations with Li-Young Lee*, edited by Earl Ingersoll, BOA, 2006.

xii "A 1962 Sylvia Plath Interview with Peter Orr," https://www.modern americanpoetry.org/content/1962-sylvia-plath-interview-peter-orr.

xiii https://www.modernamericanpoetry.org/content/1962-sylvia-plath-interview-peter-orr.

xiv Winterson, p. 105.

xv Hirshfield, Jane, *Nine Gates*, Harper Perennial, 1998, p. 37.

xvi Glück, Louise, *Proofs and Theories*, Ecco, 1995, p. 45.

xvii Ruefle, p. 15.

xviii Manguso, Sarah, *The Two Kinds of Decay*, Picador, 2008, p. 184.

xix Zucker, Rachel, and Richard Siken, "Episode 52: Richard Siken," in *Commonplace Podcast*, https://www.commonpodcast.com/home/2018/5/23/episode-52-richard-siken.

xx "Bird intelligence," Wikipedia, https://en.wikipedia.org/wiki/Bird_intelligence.

xxi https://en.wikipedia.org/wiki/Bird_intelligence.

xxii Park Hong, Cathy, *Minor Feelings*, One World/Random House, 2020, p. 188.

xxiii Sontag, Susan, *As Consciousness Is Harnessed to Flesh: Diaries 1964-1980*, edited by David Rieff, Penguin UK, 2012.

xxiv Krug, Nora, *Belonging: A German Reckons with History and Home*, Scribner, 2019.

xxv Macdonald, Helen, *H Is for Hawk*, Grove Press, p. 199.

xxvi Simic, Charles, *Dime-Store Alchemy: The Art of Joseph Cornell*, New York Review of Books, 2011.

xxvii Mandel'shtam, Osip, *The Collected Critical Prose and Letters*, edited by Jane Gary Harris, Collins Harvill, 1991.

xxviii Pavlović, p. 57.

xxix Rilke, Rainer Maria, *The Notebooks of Malte Laurids Brigge*, Penguin, 2009.

xxx Pavlović, p. 274.

xxxi Pavlović, p. 274.

xxxii Winterson, *Art Objects: Essays on Ecstasy and Effrontery*, Vintage, 1995.

The photo of Broadway is from the New York Public Library Digital Collections, taken by George L. Balgue, 1914.

Acknowledgments

I have tried to recreate events, locales, and conversations from my memories of them. In some instances I have changed the names of individuals and places, and I have changed some identifying characteristics and details, such as physical qualities, occupations, and locations, to protect the privacy of people involved.

Thank you to the editors of the following journals in which some of these pieces first appeared, sometimes in different forms.

Avidly: "Dear Grandmother: Today I found a Certificate of Marriage"

Copper Nickel: "Dear Mother: I have so many questions," "Dear Sister: Do you remember," "Dear Mother: Recently I found your marriage license," and "Dear C: You call me all the time"

Normal School: "Dear Daughter: Sometimes I wish," "Dear Daughters: One summer I intended," and "Dear Teacher: You were the most rigorous teacher"

ZYZZVA: "Dear Mother: I have been thinking about the Chinese restaurant"

Thank you to Milkweed Editions and all the good people there, especially Daniel Slager for believing in this book, and Mary Austin Speaker for helping to make it beautiful. Thank you to all my friends at Copper Canyon Press who publish my poetry and support my work.

Thanks to the MacDowell Colony for the Katherine Min Fellowship and the Lannan Foundation for a Residency Fellowship. Both fellowships gave me much-needed time to work on this book.

Thank you to my friends and supporters, way too many to mention all of them here. But special thanks to Ilya Kaminsky for always being my first reader and biggest cheerleader. Thanks to G. C. Waldrep for always making me do and be better. Thanks to Dana Levin for helping this book through multiple versions and for being a trusted comrade in art and life. Thanks to Dean Rader for helping to make this book better and for our friendship. Thanks to Monica Ong for your good eye and help on this manuscript—what a joy it's been to exchange work with you.

Thanks to Rick Barot, Paisley Rekdal, and Mark Wunderlich for the good laughs and for pushing me to be a better writer, reader, and thinker. Thanks to friends and supporters such as Michael Wiegers, Ann Townsend, Van Khanna, Ada Limón, Blas Falconer, Jaswinder Bolina, Matthew Zapruder, Jen Chang, Cecily Parks, Ismail Muhammad, Cyrus Cassells, Dan Handler, Elline Lipkin, Nan Cohen, Maggie Smith, David Baker, John Gallaher, Wayne Miller, Liza Voges, the late Jon Tribble, and so many more.

Thanks to my family for always doing the difficult work of being around an obsessive creative person. And thanks to my mother and father for doing their very best.

Issac Fitzgerald

VICTORIA CHANG is the author of *Dear Memory*. Her poetry books include *OBIT*, *Barbie Chang*, *The Boss*, *Salvinia Molesta*, and *Circle*. *OBIT* received the Los Angeles Times Book Prize, the Anisfield-Wolf Book Award, and the PEN/Voelcker Award; it was also a finalist for the National Book Critics Circle Prize and the Griffin Poetry Prize, and was long-listed for the National Book Award. She is also the author of a children's picture book, *Is Mommy?*, illustrated by Marla Frazee and named a *New York Times* Notable Book, and a middle grade novel, *Love, Love*. She has received a Guggenheim Fellowship, a Sustainable Arts Foundation Fellowship, the Poetry Society of America's Alice Fay Di Castagnola Award, a Pushcart Prize, a Lannan Residency Fellowship, and a Katherine Min MacDowell Colony Fellowship. She lives in Los Angeles and is the program chair of Antioch University's low-residency MFA program.

milkweed
editions

Founded as a nonprofit organization in 1980, Milkweed Editions is an independent publisher. Our mission is to identify, nurture, and publish transformative literature, and build an engaged community around it.

Milkweed Editions is based in Bdé Óta Othúŋwe (Minneapolis) within Mní Sota Makhóčhe, the traditional homeland of the Dakhóta people. Residing here since time immemorial, Dakhóta people still call Mní Sota Makhóčhe home, with four federally recognized Dakhóta nations and many more Dakhóta people residing in what is now the state of Minnesota. Due to continued legacies of colonization, genocide, and forced removal, generations of Dakhóta people remain disenfranchised from their traditional homeland. Presently, Mní Sota Makhóčhe has become a refuge and home for many Indigenous nations and peoples, including seven federally recognized Ojibwe nations. We humbly encourage our readers to reflect upon the historical legacies held in the lands they occupy.

milkweed.org

Interior design by Mary Austin Speaker and Tijqua Daiker
Typeset in Caslon

Adobe Caslon Pro was created by Carol Twombly
for Adobe Systems in 1990. Her design was inspired by
the family of typefaces cut by the celebrated engraver
William Caslon I, whose family foundry served
England with clean, elegant type from the early
Enlightenment through the turn of the
twentieth century.